Letters from the Hearth

Fr. Dan Madigan

ISBN 0-9715669-0-9
Copyright © 2001. This book is published in celebration of the twenty-fifth anniversary
of The Sacramento Food Bank Services.

Photographs by Rochelle Pastor, Tom & Sally Myers, et al.
(detail photo credits on page 288)
Interior layout and design by Silvest Morris
Cover art by JC Evans Communications

Sacramento Food Bank Services
(916) 456-1980
www.sfbs.org

Printed in the United States of America by Fruitridge Printing & Lithograph
Sacramento, California

ACKNOWLEDGEMENTS

I gratefully acknowledge the following for their help in putting together this book:
Eileen Elfsten, Mary Alice Hendricks, Richard White, Silvest Morris, Nona McGlashan, Bonnie Ward,
Richard Fisher, Cynthia Yelland, The Sacramento Bee, and all the authors of the quotations used in the book.

I also give special mention to:
Peter and Carole Berghuis
Sacramento Food Bank Services Board of Directors
Sacramento Food Bank Services Priests Advisory Board
Fruitridge Printing & Lithograph Inc., Sacramento

I want to express my deep thanks to Rochelle Pastor for her
unwavering support, dedication and intense energy that she has
given to the making of this book. Her photography, photographic
editing and creativity have made it possible to bring *Letters From
The Hearth* to fruition.

OUR MISSION

- Feeding the hungry
- Clothing the needy
- Housing the homeless
- Educating the illiterate
- Providing moms with guidance and their infants with formula, diapers and necessary baby items
- Furnishing seniors with a social club and a plethora of volunteer opportunities
- Furnishing all ages with a computer clubhouse which was established for SFBS by Intel
- Providing early childhood education and youth services
- Strengthening families through a program of ethics and self-esteem

OUR PHILOSOPHY

Adherence to the principles of:
- God our Almighty Father
- Christ His beloved Son
- Saints who practiced the heavenly message of social justice and compassion

INTRODUCTION

by Father Dan Madigan

Sacramento Food Bank Services celebrated its twenty-fifth anniversary on January 17, 2001. Since then I have been asked by several people to write a history of its formation and some of its ensuing accomplishments.

Taking the easy way out I decided to tell its history through the hundred plus letters I have written to its supporters over the years.

However, before jumping into this task I would like to say a few words about some places that played a big part in the formation of SFBS. These places are Del Paso Heights, the Fabulous Forties, Oak Park, Immaculate Conception Church and the Arata Bros. store.

On coming to this country from Ireland, I was immediately planted in Del Paso Heights. I lived among, worked with, and was an integral part of that community from the mid-sixties to early seventies. I got to know all about the residents of that area and their daily struggle with inadequate income. The districts of Robla, Rio Linda, Elverta, McClellan Air Force Base and North Sacramento also were no stranger to me.

On leaving there I promised I would one day return and help alleviate some of the pain in Del Paso Heights. This I did in 1985. And since then, under the auspices of SFBS, we have operated a food outlet there that feeds approximately 200 families a day.

Our headquarters is a triple-wide mobile unit which has been irreverently referred to by a local entrepreneur as "Fr. Dan's Trailer Rancho." Nevertheless this building has done the job and will continue to do so until we come up with something better. Abandoning the people of this area is something SFBS has no intention of doing.

In 1972 I was assigned to Sacred Heart Church, which serves the Fabulous Forties area of Sacramento. I got to see how other people lived and also discovered that these wonderful folks were more than willing to help the poor provided that a mechanism for doing so was made available.

In 1976 I applied for and was appointed to Immaculate Conception Church in Oak Park. When this church, which stands on the corner of 32nd Street and Broadway, was built in 1916, it was surrounded by an affluent, residential neighborhood. By the time I got there it was different.

In the 1960's Oak Park was mutilated by the invasion of two intercepting freeways. Blocks of gracious living flanked by streets of established enterprises were eliminated. The freeways themselves, and their huge cloverleaf over Broadway, took out hundreds of homes. Many people were dislocated. Many more just moved away. Oak Park gradually slid into the inner-city, multi-racial neighborhood that I found when I moved there in January 1976. Its story is truly a "Cinderella" in reverse. Riches to rags.

For the following fourteen years Immaculate Conception Church was my home. While there I founded SFBS. Later the Arata building would become its new home. The Arata name is legendary in Sacramento. The famous Arata Bros. Grocery was operated by Charlie Arata for at least 50 years off Broadway on the corner of 34th Street and 3rd Avenue. It closed in the mid-seventies but sprang back to life again in November 1987, when it opened up as Sacramento Food Bank Services. Outlined is a history of the Arata family which was written in the spring of 1988 by Nona McGlashan, a local author and at that time a very active volunteer at Sacramento Food Bank Services.

"The three Arata brothers, Andrew N., Frank L., and Charles L., created Sacramento's first grocery store chain, famous throughout the valley for at least six decades. The dedication of their Oak Park store at 34th off Broadway as Arata Bros. Center not only engraves the Arata name on our city's living history, but also memorializes the charity and responsibility these brothers always showed the 'neighbor' in need.

This was notably true of the youngest, Charles, who operated the Oak Park store. A bachelor all his life, he was a kindly man who always wore bib overalls, fed the pigeons, and was a soft touch for any worthy cause. Charitable organizations could depend on discounts for hot dogs and other picnic supplies. Enormously popular and patronized by shoppers from a hundred miles away, the Oak Park store's profits would have been much higher but for Charlie's 'backdoor' charities. Former employees recall that once, when picketed by union members and rain began to fall, he outfitted each picketer in rain gear at his own expense. They continued picketing against him – with smiling faces.

Nevertheless, Charlie could be a strict employer who permitted no loitering on the job. He demanded responsible hard work, the virtue that led him and his brothers to distinguished success. From that day in 1907 when Andrew, 25, the oldest, called the others together for a conference on where they, as a family group, were going, their determination and vision never faltered.

Sons of Lorenzo J. and Nellie Lavezzo Arata, natives of Amador County, the boys were born near the mining town of Jackson. Andrew, the firstborn, married Elfrena Matson when he was 21 and began learning business management at Jackson's leading store, Marre's. By the time he summoned his younger brothers to confer, he had his eye on the larger town of Sacramento, some 50 miles away, and he had in mind a store of his own with brother Frank as partner. Charlie, still in his teens, could learn from the bottom up and age his way into partnership, if he so wished.

Theirs was the warmth of the 'family store' with that human touch and kindly concern rarely known today. During the Great Depression of the thirties, they traded home garden vegetables and fruits for bacon, beans and flour, watchful that needy families had such staples. They were the first to start the "cash and carry" system, allowing the customer to fill a basket from bins and shelves and pay cash for groceries at the check stand. This was imitated by other stores and is the only practice today.

Andrew, slowed by illness but active, died in 1962 at age 79. Frank continued to carry on in the business only a few years longer. He, too, was now along in years. He died in 1968 at 81, having sold most of the Arata holdings. Charlie alone remained with the Oak Park store, which he sold to the Eagle Thrifty Drug and Grocers of Reno, Nevada, in the early 1970's. The Arata magic gone, the new firm lasted only two years, a bitter disappointment to Charlie, who died in 1976, aged 85. His Oak Park building, which occupied, as today, most of a city block, was gifted to McGeorge School of Law.

An era had ended but the brothers' love for Sacramento would not die with it. This love was expressed by Andrew Arata in an interview when he said: "Every cent we have made both in our retail business and our wholesale house we have invested right here in Sacramento. This is our home town, the city we love. It has been good to us. We feel it is only simple justice that the money we make should be invested, every cent of it, here at home. That principle will always guide us."

All the brothers became millionaires, but remained unpretentious. To the end they cleaved to the values, principles and goals of their original youthful vision. Frank's will, dated August 1, 1963, instructed the trustees of his estate to invest profits "For charitable, scientific, literary, religious or other educational purposes for the prevention of cruelty to children." According to the will, the fund was to be known as the Arata Brothers Trust. It seems like poetic justice that their Oak Park facility should become a haven for the hungry and a source of ministry to the poor.

And what of the Arata women, that devoted corps of cousins and nieces without whom the whole structure would have been sorely weakened? The Lavezzo "girls" as they were always called, both Nellie and Jeanette, are active and well, in their early 90's. They still live in Sacramento, as does Andrew's daughter, Dorothy Arata Bliss. Her sister, Ellena Arata Sewell, widow of Abner Sewell, who owned a chain grocery business throughout Nevada, lives in Reno. They are the heroines of a happy story that, with the dedication of Arata Social Services promises to have an ongoing happy ending.

With youth, enthusiasm and courage but no real capital assets behind them, they acquired a makeshift store on 12ʰ and J streets. Old-timers described it as 'an old shed built over' for their use. Working day and night to make it presentable, they somehow stocked it with staples and fresh produce and, in 1908, nervously opened its doors to a responsive public. Honest weight, fair prices and courteous service – the brothers 'guiding business principles, were soon to attract and hold a growing stream of customers.

Within remarkably few years a new building was built on the site of the humble first store. Andrew, always the leader, equipped himself with a correspondence course from San Francisco's Heald Business College, which he passed with flying colors. In 1910 he recruited his cousin, Nellie Lavezzo, 17, to work in the office. She, too, took a correspondence business course with colors equally flying. Andrew would soon add her sister, Jeanette, to his office staff and, in due course, his own daughters, Dorothy and Ellena. All the girls were to devote many years to the family business.

In 1913 the brothers were ready to branch out. They established the Oak Park store at 34ʰ Street and 3ʳᵈ Avenue, a prosperous residential area. This was to become Charlie's province all his working life. With cousin Jeanette for office and general help, he took over the management in 1917 after two years in the U.S. Navy.

Three more retail stores followed in steady progression – one in North Sacramento, another in the rapidly growing eastern section, and the last downtown, at 16ʰ and S streets. By the end of the 1920's, Arata Brothers owned the only grocery chain in the valley and also the most successful business of its kind in the West, according to a national magazine.

It was time, the firm decided, to build a wholesale house, separate and distinct from the retail stores, one to serve the entire valley. This they did at 20ʰ and R streets . Valley Wholesale Grocery was described by a contemporary as a "vast warehouse, with massive concrete flooring, admirable lighting and ventilation systems, where tons and tons of food from all parts of the world were stored." In the center of incessant activity sits Andrew Arata, the directing genius of this partnership. Frank Arata, too, was recalled as "a man in a blue cotton jacket working the Arata magic within the whirlpool of busy enterprise, never too busy to turn for a moment and wait on the most humble of customers."

SACRAMENTO FOOD BANK SERVICES - TODAY

- Handles much more than food.
- It is a comprehensive social service agency.
- It is a grass-roots community-supported organization.
- Ninety-three percent of its needed income comes from Sacramentans.
- Ninety-five percent of its staff are volunteers.
- Salaried staff provide guidance to the volunteer staff.
- It distributes fish and teaches people how to fish.
- Each of its programs advocates self-reliance and private initiative.
- It is a very strong advocate of the mentoring practice.

The following are its programs and the years they were founded:

1976	Food Outlets	1992	Mother/Baby Program
1983	Sunday Lunch	1993	Senior Bridge Builders
1988	Clothes Closet	1998	The P.L.A.C.E. (Parent Learning and Children Education)
1989	Community Learning Center	2000	Women's Wisdom Project
1991	Havens Transitional Housing	2000	Intel Computer Clubhouse

Recently in seeking summary statements of accomplishments for the year 2000 from our different programs, I was very much taken by one of the statistics presented. The Mother/Baby Program stated that during this past year it had collaborated with 320 agencies.

This statistic took my mind back to the year 1983. Sacramento had received $370,000 from the Federal Emergency Management Agency (FEMA) to feed the local poor. I decided to throw my hat in the ring. What I experienced then made me shy away from bureaucracies ever since. Nona McGlashan, in a letter to the Catholic Herald, describes what took place:

Editor:

Recently the Sacramento Bee featured a report titled: "Food and Shelter Board Funnels $370,000 to 15 agencies." I attended the allocation meeting and, since the report mentioned Father Dan Madigan's "heated criticisms" of the board's decisions, I would like to give his many supporters a lay observer's impressions.

Father Madigan's record in feeding the poor is well known. For over seven years the community has seen the hungry at Immaculate Conception's Food Locker window – and now, in ever increasing numbers. In March, I.C. began serving free hot meals on a once-a-month basis in the apparent hope of making it a weekly event when practicable. When these federal emergency funds became available, it seemed to be the answer to his hot meal program and Father Madigan applied for a grant.

His request was denied. Instead, the Food Locker was given a token grant – and this was contingent on its purchasing the food from Interfaith Service Bureau. According to the representative at the meeting, Father Madigan would have to become a member of Interfaith Service Bureau in order to buy. To this he objected strongly on grounds that he is able to buy from the fields and other sources more economically. Furthermore, he said, Interfaith has "harassed" him for years to join the agency and he felt that this was another ruse to coerce him. He therefore refused the grant, saying that although the Food Locker could naturally use the monies, it would not be coerced into joining Interfaith Service.

Hard as he fought for the hot meal program, stressing the large and growing attendance each month, the board was inflexible. To an observer, its reasons seemed full of holes. For starters, they said another agency in the neighborhood was already serving free hot meals. This turned out to be a small operation that only seats 20 people. Yet another objection of the board was that Immaculate Conception's auditorium only seats 350! Why BOTH programs could not be funded in this needy area was indeed puzzling.

Throughout the long meeting, the most vocal person at the board's table was Jim Mills, Community Planning Council director, although he was there only as a staff member. The board members themselves spoke very little, so much so that I wondered if Mills had actually made the decisions and the members were only vaguely aware of the reasons for them. Father Madigan repeatedly, without success, tried to draw response from Mehl Simmons, County Welfare's deputy director, reminding him that I.C.'s Food Locker had taken care of 6,000 families sent by the county over the years.

The Catholic Social Service's director, one of the three members on the recommending committee, was conspicuously silent.

I left the meeting feeling that neither justice nor the interests of the poor were uppermost in the decisions of what seemed to me a weak, confused board. However, it could not have been too confused since, as the Bee reported, two-thirds of the total fund went to its own members projects.

After that experience I came to the conclusion that reliance on government keeps all in bondage. And that eating from its trough destroys all initiative.

Then and there I decided that SFBS would remain a grass-roots organization. Sacramentans would feed Sacramentans. And they would do it with their own money and with their own hands and energy.

And it worked and continues to do so 25 years later. Ninety-five percent of staff are volunteers. Ninety-three percent of our income comes from the pockets of our friends, the Sacramento community.

Father Dan and Dorothy Arata Bliss

Dear Friends:

Sacramento's poverty is a well-kept secret. Distant and sensational problems seem to attract more media attention. A six-year stint in Del Paso Heights and ten years in the Oak Park area have shown me that hunger, poverty and dependence are not limited to Third World countries. The lack of quality of life in our own backyard needs to be brought out into the open.

Daily I watch the less fortunate line up along our food locker's chain link fence. As they await their meager rations, I study their faces, tense with anxiety, twisted with frustration and saddled with pain. I can even categorize these unfortunate people for you. Standing there in collective alienation are the mentally ill, the chronically unemployed, the unskilled workers, the physically and socially handicapped, the illiterate and many, many moms with their ragged, unkempt children.

At the time of my ordination in 1964, it was customary for the newly ordained to single out a few lines of Scripture, place it on an ordination card and make it one's overall goal for life. The quotation I chose was: *The Spirit of the Lord is upon me; He has anointed me and sent me to preach the Gospel to the poor, to restore the broken-hearted.* Oftentimes since I have felt that the Lord really took me at my word. For the past twenty years He has given me the privilege of a ringside seat among the poor.

So with the philosophy of **It's better to light a candle than curse the darkness**, we are now operating a food locker and soup kitchen in Oak Park. We are reaching thousands of people and are blessed with several hundred volunteers, who like the compassionate Christ have a special soft spot in their hearts for the poor. Like Him, these generous people believe in defending the poor, protecting the weak and liberating the oppressed.

Yes, friends, it is not the number of years that we spend between the cradle and the grave that matters. It's the way we live them. The amount of good that we get into them. The things we do that better and brighten the lives of others. After all, we are not cold vegetables growing in the field with other vegetables. We are human beings rubbing shoulders with each other and, hopefully, acting as Christ wants us to act. Please consider giving us a hand, and while doing so keep in mind that "Christ has no hands but our hands to do His work today."

May Almighty God bless you and reward you for your goodness.

With every good wish,

Fr. Dan Madigan

Dear Friends:

Even though more Americans were hungry last winter than at any time since the Great Depression, public outcry has reached only a minimal level. This is so because few people fully realize what is taking place in regard to the poor. A greater public sympathetic understanding of why people become or stay poor is needed. Some believe that the poor are somehow themselves to blame for their poverty. Others claim that many of the poor are con artists who rip off food lockers and cheese "giveaways" while they own fancy cars. A segment may very well be guilty of this. But the vast majority who call on us for food are truly hurting and it is about them I speak here.

A very large number of those who come to our food locker/soup kitchen are, in my opinion, chronically disturbed. Their mental illness is immediately evident. Character and personality disorders render them unable to cope with the demands of daily life. Some can be heard muttering to themselves or answering voices that only they can hear. Others would willingly share their delusion and hallucination if they could find listeners. All seem to be crying out for appropriate psychiatric help that apparently does not exist for them.

Another definable group at the food locker gate is the alcoholics. Usually they are unattached, middle-aged men. Alcohol is their central frame of reference, impermanence is their way of life. They get kicked out of hotels, frequent the missions and Salvation Army, sleep out in weeds and occasionally spend a night in jail. As a rule they stay in their own areas, for they are well aware of the stigma they carry as "bums." A hostile world awaits them if they emerge from there. They have a deep sense of personal failure and have usually abandoned any reasonable hope of recreating themselves. Alcohol is their only friend, providing them with some measure of euphoria and optimism, dulling the loneliness, unhappiness and sense of social inadequacy. This type of living eventually takes its toll and can be easily seen from their tattered clothing, their absence of self-esteem and their health problems. I find it difficult to believe that human beings who are reduced to foraging in dumpsters, **collecting aluminum cans** and selling blood for existence are taking advantage of food lockers.

Next come the neighborhood parents who are often accompanied by their ragged, unkempt children. Born poor, they have yet to escape the clutch of poverty. Their most determined efforts to raise themselves are defeated by the miserable conditions in which they are obliged to live. Their rents are excessive, their neighborhoods degrading, their public amenities inferior; their surroundings discourage any initiative. Day after day the poor keep coming to our food locker. I have watched them for nine years now, and the only difference I see of late is the huge increase in numbers. The line is always made up of the same type of people: The mentally ill, the alcoholics, the chronically unemployed, the unskilled workers, the deserted wives, the very ill, the physically and socially handicapped, the street people, the badly housed, the ex-prisoners, the educationally deprived.

What are we to do? St. Paul stood by uninvolved as people stoned the martyr Stephen. He spent his life regretting it. As followers of the Lord, the care of the poor and the oppressed are our personal responsibility. We are all responsible when people suffer from hunger, cold, oppression and hatred. We cannot be indifferent. We cannot be apathetic. We cannot stand idly by. We are not powerless. We can make a difference!

With every good wish to you,

Fr. Dan Madigan

18

Dear Friends:

Our Lord said, *"Blessed are they who have not seen and yet believed."*

I think Edwin Meese's recent statement indicates that he has not seen poverty. He lives in an affluent neighborhood, his friends are wealthy and well educated. He sees no poverty and, therefore, basically does not believe in its existence.

I have always been amazed that **areas of poverty and affluence can exist within a short distance of each other** in a city and still have no interaction. Both groups move in their own worlds and are worlds apart. The wealthy have no reason to go into the ghetto, and even if they did, they would feel like lost souls there. The same would be true for a poor person in a rich neighborhood. Very few people are blessed with the opportunity to become sufficiently acquainted with both worlds, to move in both with ease.

Poverty does exist in Sacramento and I see it on a daily basis – poor, hungry, victimized people, the ones Our Lord spoke of in the Beatitudes. These are the people I see here every day. Many are angry, broken and disturbed, and are extremely difficult to work with. When our Blessed Lord called us to be the defenders of the poor, protectors of the weak and liberators of the oppressed, He was not asking for any small task but for every ounce of energy and good will we could muster.

So may the good Lord bless you and imbue you with His own favorite text from the prophet Isaiah: *The Spirit of the Lord is upon me. He has anointed me and sent me to preach the Gospel to the poor and to restore the brokenhearted.*

With every good blessing and every best wish to you.

Fr. Dan Madigan

Dear Friends:

Occasionally I stand outside the dispensing window and talk with the people who wait in line there for food. I find it impossible to categorize them or even their attitudes. They come from all walks of life – men and women of all ages, races and cultures. Now and then I see a few who are happy, life-loving, even boisterous. But on the whole, their faces are tense with anxiety, twisted with inner turmoil or saddened by one or another of the many kinds of pain.

Here are desperate, disappointed people with no ties, few roots and frequently no shelter. Loneliness is prevalent among them and some have even chosen to walk alone – like **those who bring their whole world stuffed into a shopping cart** that has become their mobile home. These are people of loss – loss of hearing, of health, of self-esteem. All they know is menial work, for they are also people of lacks – lack of education, lack of skills. Alcohol has become the escape of many.

While I stand in line with these people, I am keenly aware of a segment among them that has seen social workers and programs come and go without giving them any deep down help or understanding. This has apparently made them quite callous.

Sometimes I make it a point to stand on the other side of the window, looking over the shoulder of the volunteer who receive requests and evaluate needs. Of all volunteer tasks, I am sure that the one who sits at the window has the most difficult. For how is one to cope with the litany of disappointment, anxiety, pain and despair, day after day, month in and month out? How does one stay highly motivated? How can one remain zealous and not burn out under the stress?

I guess hard work done with conviction and enthusiasm will never cause stress or burnout. I am sure we create stress for ourselves. And I think we cause stress for ourselves at the window when we begin to feel we must try to change significantly the people we meet there. There is no possible way we can change them. We can only change our own evaluation of them. If we try to imagine that they are drowning in a lake and that we are rescuers who throw a rope, pull them out and put them on solid ground for at lest a little while, then perhaps we will feel our job is meaningful and that we are accomplishing a great deal.

However, if we ask ourselves why these people are drowning, why they are in the lake, why they are outside the window, why they lie, giving false names and information to get more food than they are entitled to, such questions can cause us tremendous frustration. We can easily understand why they lie to get more food. But once a volunteer goes heavily into the "why" of their need to beg in this great country of ours, or the "why" of their inadequacies, then that volunteer should probably move to another aspect of the Food Locker service. The window will become far too stressful.

Many times I've asked myself if it would be more Christian to fight for people's rights than give someone a basket of food. Is it more Christian to attack the sources of suffering than to relieve the suffering itself? These are big questions that are nice to ponder while sitting on a commission of social concern. But I think these questions are above and beyond reality for us. The real question is what are we doing about the poor here and now? How are we touching their lives? Of course, there should not be any hungry people in this country. The point is, there are. They are here. They are in Oak Park. They are outside the window looking in.

I believe no sane person would line up and wait outside a food locker window for a few loaves of bread or can of beans if they had money in their pocket or the wherewithal to live comfortably. I will not believe

that, I have never believed it. And I do not feel that anyone has ever taken advantage of our food locker. I see very little excuse therefore to refuse anyone, and I feel we have never been "ripped off". If they give false information in trying to obtain food for themselves and their families, can we say they are not justified? If the people at our window tell us white lies, I think worse things could happen.

From an administrative point of view, I am in the dual position of **looking through both sides of the window.** I have never experienced what the person feels who waits in line. I have been spared that. And I think it must be experienced in order to understand, deep down, what it is really like. I can, however, sympathize and identify with the volunteer at the window, whose stresses are very real. I only hope that, as time goes by, **I will identify more and more with the person outside looking in.**

God bless you and take care of yourself,

Fr. Dan Madigan

O, God, when I have food,
help me to remember the hungry.
When I have work,
help me to remember the jobless.
When I have a warm home,
help me to remember the homeless.
When I am without pain,
help me to remember those who suffer.
And remembering,
help me to destroy my complacency
and bestir my compassion.
Make me concerned enough to help,
by word and deed, those who cry out
for what we take for granted.
                    Author unknown

Dear Friends:

It is easy to be nice to those who send us thank-you cards, shake our hand and tell us how helpful we have been. These are usually our family members, friends and neighbors, co-workers perhaps – all people of our own kind.

It's not so easy to be nice to the ungrateful; the boring or burdensome; the winos and bums; the embarrassingly down-at-the-heel panhandlers or others below us on the scale of "class". **And yet these are the ones the Lord told us to be nice to.**

Nowhere did Christ say what we do for the prosperous and popular we do for Him. It is in the weak, the sick, the sinners, the losers, specifically in THEM, He told us to look for Him and serve Him. And so, in the late evening when the rectory doorbell sends me down the stairs to look through the peephole, I know I am going to have a choice to make. When I see that a man on the porch is not a parishioner but a shabby disheveled street person, I can do one of two things. I can tiptoe back up the stairs, pretending no one is home and my visitor will soon walk away. On the other hand, if I open the door, street people are never the most appealing to deal with. They wear a hodge-podge of odds and ends fished from trash bins and often they reek of cheap booze, sweat and urine. They rarely express themselves well and their awkward speech and manners varies from servility to rudeness.

Yet here waits a human being in need of almost everything – a bath, clean clothes, food, a place to sleep and, most of all, an encouraging word. It would be so easy to pretend I'm out. Choice stares me in the face.

In all honesty, I must say that when I open the door, which I do, it is more often than not a real act of faith, blind trust that Jesus meant what He said about finding Him in this specific "least" brother. It is hard sometimes to see Him in eyes haunted by rejections, fears, suspicions, even hatreds. But I know that I must try.

May the Good Lord bless you,

Fr. Dan Madigan

Dear Friends:

I believe I learned sensitivity toward the poor from my mother's example. I was the eight of nine children around the table, growing up in rural Ireland.

We were neither rich nor poor, but we learned about poverty from Mom and Dad, who had seen much of it as children.

In Ireland we had tinkers, as we call them, instead of street people, who begged at our door. Only once did I ever see Mom turn anyone away and I'll never forget her remorse. A tinker knocked when she was very busy and rushed for time. She sent him packing abruptly without a morsel. After a few thoughtful moments, out the door **she ran, chasing him down the road and calling him back to a hot meal.** She always believed that any poor person who knocked at the door was sent by divine Providence and who can say she was not right?

My Leader, Christ, is a lovable but difficult Man to work for. He tells me that the number of years between cradle and grave doesn't matter as much as input of thought and care for others. It is not good enough, He tells me, just to live out my life diligently or even successfully. The only failure in His eyes lies in shrugging off the "losers." Indifference to the poor is the measure of self-centeredness and lovelessness, He would have me know.

No, it is not easy to love the unlovable, the un-nice, the people who struggle along the years as the least of His brothers and ours. But we have to try. If we perform caring actions our sensitivity will grow. With sensitivity comes understanding, and with understanding, brotherly love such as amazed the Roman world two thousand years ago. *"See how these Christians love one another,"* they said. May our own world today say the same of us.

May the Good Lord bless you,

Fr. Dan Madigan

Dear Friends:

One need not be much of a churchgoer to be familiar with the Bible's story of the multiplication of loaves and fishes.

It has been suggested to me recently that the multiplication could have been worked in two different ways, equally miraculous. The first way is the one I have always understood from the Gospel. By His divine power, Jesus simply made the bread and fishes multiply.

But another way could have been thus: When He blessed the food and told His disciples to distribute it, His blessing touched the minds and hearts of the crowd. They had come to the hillside singly or in small groups whose only bond was common curiosity. Suddenly, something happened. Each one turned to look into the face of the stranger beside him or her and saw – community. Family. And the little hoards of food they'd brought along for self and friends began to be passed to people who had become, in a flash of insight, neighbors instead of strangers. It was a miracle of the heart. A saint has said it is easier for God to heal broken bones than to change the human heart. That would make this way more miraculous than any other.

I need your help to make this kind of miracle happen here in our own Sacramento community. You and I can't feed the world, but **together and with God's help we can care for our city's hungry people.**

We now operate five food lockers and two soup kitchens. We are located in the poverty areas of Oak Park, Del Paso Heights, Meadowview and Rancho Cordova. We are blessed with hundreds of dedicated volunteers who, like Him, believe in defending the poor, protecting the weak and liberating the oppressed.

Please help us. Without your help no miracle is possible, for the "multiplication" must go on as long as a Sacramento man, woman or child suffers need. Remember the food your gift provides feeds not only bodies but also souls. With hope. With self-esteem. And with a knowledge that someone truly cares. The poor will bless you. God will bless you.

With every good wish,

Fr. Dan Madigan

Dear Friends:

Bonnie Ward of the Sacramento Union wrote the following article on June 28. I felt that she captured what we are doing very well, so I decided to make her article my letter for this month. As she points out, we have brought the fundraising campaign nearly three-fourths of the way toward its $1 million goal.

When the Rev. Dan Madigan announced last winter that he wanted to raise $1 million for a new home for the Oak Park Food Bank, even his closest aides thought he was a little crazy.

"But $700,000 later, he's not so crazy." Said John Healey, Madigan's right-hand man and new director of the Food Bank.

A savvy fundraising expert, multitudes of volunteers, and "some help from above" have brought the fundraising campaign nearly three-fourths of the way to its $1 million goal.

But now the final hurdle is about to begin.

From July 7 – 14, an army of volunteers – coordinated by Madigan's Immaculate Conception Church -will descend upon the homes of more than 2,000 Sacramentans who have previously donated time or money to the Food Bank.

Armed with small green pledge cards and a strong desire to help the poor, the volunteers will stage their final fundraising assault in the battle to move the crowded Food Bank to an upgraded, expanded facility.

The Food Bank's new home is to be a 30,000 square-foot warehouse at 3333 Third Avenue that once housed the Arata Market.

Strolling through the massive vacant warehouse, Healey talks with the enthusiasm of a new home-buyer who has found a dream home.

"Over here we'll distribute clothes," Healey said. "And here," he said gesturing to a huge wall of walk-in freezers, "we'll keep all our refrigerated food."

The building stands in stark contract to the makeshift, overcrowded distribution site a few blocks away at the church.

There, food is stored in every nook and cranny from the church basement to the rectory. A refrigerated railroad car doubles as a walk-in freezer, volunteers work in a cramped trailer and old semi-truck trailers filled with rice and beans are scattered about.

From 10 a.m. to 2 p.m. weekdays the needy line up to receive the sackfuls of rice, flour, corn and other staples that will stretch their food budget a few days more.

Their stream is steady and their numbers ever increasing. Last year the Food Bank and satellite food lockers in Del Paso Heights, Meadowview and Rancho Cordova gave food to 250,535 people – more than half of them children.

"The concept I hear is that these are street people, winos that come to our kitchens," Madigan said. "But actually, the majority of our people are families with children, the elderly and people from single-parent households. It's time someone started roaring that from the house tops."

Madigan, described by associates as a workaholic, dreams of expanding the Food Bank to include a medical clinic, clothing outlet and counseling service.

Plans for an expanded daily soup kitchen were dropped – to church officials' chagrin – after community members protested that it would attract transients from throughout Sacramento.

(The once-a-week soup kitchen will remain in its present location at the church grounds.)

Despite that setback, church officials remain enthusiastic about the Food Bank's impending move.

Healey said the building has already been purchased through a $700,000 loan from the Diocese of Sacramento.

The church will repay the loan with $708,000 in cash and pledges it has received, although another $300,000 is needed to do the necessary remodeling.

Enter **Charles Sylva**, *a real estate agent who has taken up Madigan's cause.*

Madigan credits Sylva with opening doors to the business community that have brought in major donors – including a single contribution of $100,000. "I would never have been able to attempt it without him," Madigan said.

For more information on donating or working as a volunteer call 452-1980.

Thank you, Bonnie, for your article. Sacramentans, please remember this is your project. It's one of Sacramentans taking care of their own.

With every good wish,

Fr. Dan Madigan

Dear Friends:

Many people find the daily grind of work very difficult to bear. They look forward to retirement with great excitement.

Retirement is supposed to be a wonderful experience. No work. No worries. Lots and lots of leisure. Sometimes it truly works like this. Many times not. The reason for this is that it cuts people from their moorings and leaves them floundering around in a kind of no-man's land.

Over the years many new retirees have shared with me their first reactions. Emotional trauma of no longer being needed. A noticeable decrease of power, influence and respect. Deep loneliness and grief felt from sudden severance with workmates.

Some of these same retirees have deep fears and anxieties about many possible scenarios. Pauperization due to fixed incomes and inflationary costs. Incapacitation due to chronic disease. Danger of no option institutionalization. Rest homes, dehumanizing existence. Bereavement and loss of terminally ill spouse. Carrying with them daily the brand of dilapidation, boredom and disengagement.

Experience teaches us that when communication is low, fear is always high. Segregation, fear and hostility are synonymous. Exclusion as a protection is not only a fearful and lonely game but also one that is both common and rampant today. Leisure towns and gated communities are springing up all over the country.

When I look back at my own rural upbringing and compare it with our sophisticated way of living today, I realize what's happening. We have become totally impersonalized – a license plate, a social security number, our name spelled wrong on a computer list, a voice at the far end of the telephone. We seem to have no existence today without an ID card, a driver's license, a Master Charge, or some other equally valuable piece of plastic. It's no wonder then that this type of thinking sweeps us along so easily and turns us into weak prey for schizophrenia.

What is needed to right the situation? What is missing? More fences, more jails, more security? Certainly not. Individual interaction, irrespective of age, is what is needed. We need to get off the conveyor belt approach and try to view the situation through the other person's eyes.

St. Francis of Assisi gave us good advice when he said: *"Grant that I may not so much seek to be understood as to understand."* We all seem to be making the same mistake – we see the forest but miss the trees; we see the crowd but miss the person. We need to slow down. Nothing is more important than person-to-person contact. **The complete acceptance of another is absolutely essential before any kind of decent communication begins.**

In order to do this there is no need to deny that differences exist. But there is a need to adopt a philosophy of refusing to let differences make a difference.

With every good wish,

Fr. Dan Madigan

Dear Friends:

In today's society everyone wants to be the boss. Everyone wants to be the top dog. Everyone wants to be the person in charge.

Abraham Lincoln said: *"Nearly all men can stand adversity. But if you want to test a man's character, give him power."*

Pilate said to Jesus: *"Do you refuse to speak to me? Do you not know that I have the power to release you and the power to crucify you?"* Jesus answered: *"You would have no power over me whatever unless it were given you from above."*

The **Great Wall of China** was built to keep out invaders. It's 1,500 miles long. It's 25 feet wide at the bottom and 15 feet at the top. It was built entirely by hand and is made of bricks and granite and filled with clay. The construction began about 221 B.C. and lasted hundreds of years. Every 300 yards of wall has a 40-foot protective tower. It is such an impressive sight it can be recognized from the moon.

Here is what Dr. Harry Emerson Fosdick had to say about it: *"The Great Wall of China is a gigantic structure which cost an immense amount of money and labor. When it was finished, it appeared impregnable. But the enemy breached it. Not by breaking it down or going around it. They did it by bribing the gatekeepers."*

So the Great Wall of China did not work. It was the human factor that failed. It was a weak link of dishonesty that gave way. Its "feet of clay" came from lack of integrity, greed and unfaithfulness.

So, friends, let's always remember it's only the good and simple and proper things we do in life that really last.

With every good wish,

Fr. Dan.

Fr. Dan Madigan

Dear Friends:

At the time of World War I a larger than life-sized statue of Christ stood at a crossroads in France, with arms outstretched. During the shelling the statue's hands were blown off. Later, a passerby wrote these very fitting words on the pedestal: ***Christ has no hands but our hands.***

True, Christ has no hands but ours to do His work. We may ignore the call, ignore the need, ignore the hurting people, but unless we get out and do the work, unless we feed those hungry people, His work will not be done.

You and I are very privileged. God has called us to help His special friends, the poor. They have a special spot in His heart and we have not only been called, but are given the opportunity to alleviate their pain at least a little. In order to persevere in what we do, however, and be happy doing it, we must keep our sights on why we do it. Our motive must be the love of God.

So, dear friends, I feel it is essential that we stop from time to time and meet together for some reflection. We need to talk, to exchange ideas and give each other support.

With that in mind I invite you to an experience of spiritual uplift and renewal which I know we will find richly rewarding.

With every good wish,

Fr. Dan Madigan

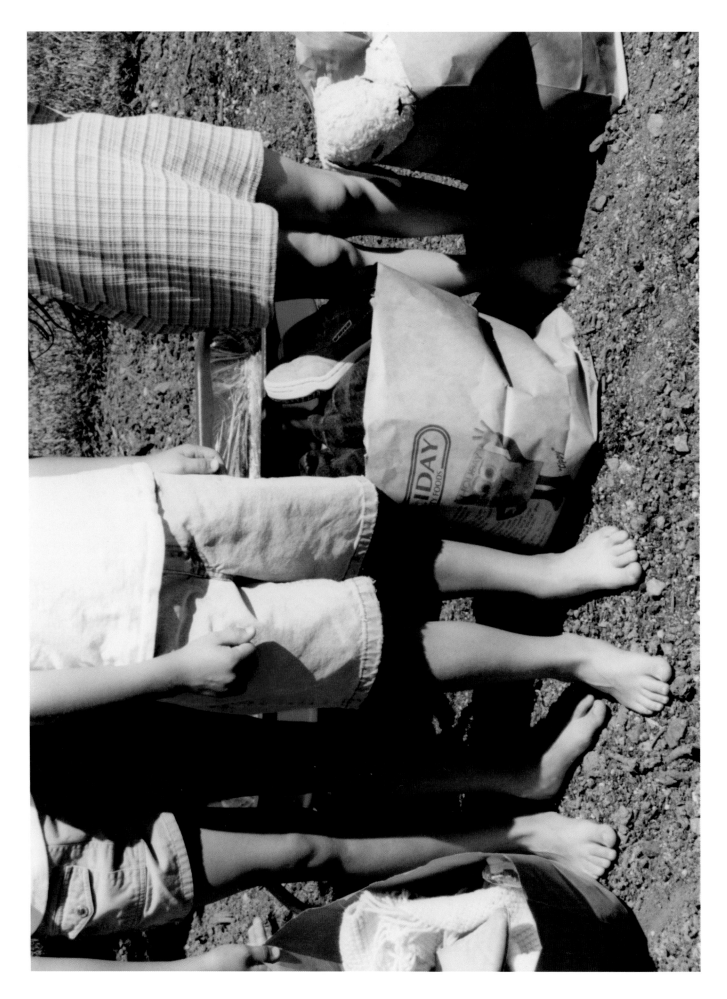

Dear Friends:

Although the food lockers close in the late afternoon, poor people's problems continue. The following is an example of the calls we receive in the night at our rectory here in Oak Park.

The urgent phone call came during an evening meeting on Food Bank business. The caller told me he was at a motel on Stockton Boulevard. He and his wife had taken in a young woman and three small children who were evicted by the motel manager. The woman was pregnant, no place to go, and could I help?

I was about to explain that I run only food programs and have nothing to do with housing. Then it struck me that I had better practice what I preach. I heard myself say, "Give me your address and room number. I'll be down to see you in an hour."

Charles Sylva went with me. We found a raunchy motel of the cheapest kind. In the dim lighting we saw the number we were looking for and a black man opened the door to our knock. His wife smiled at us in greeting and a small, obviously pregnant young woman stared at us without expression from a thin, pale face. Three toddlers, aged 3,2 and 1, lay on the bed. They each wore a diaper and nothing else.

The mother may have been 20, but her speech and manner indicated extreme immaturity and little education. She and her husband had driven from Arkansas earlier in the week. We could imagine the rest. No job. No money. Three babies needing everything only money could buy. Did the man decide the wife could do better without him? Whatever he thought, he had left her high and dry, totally adrift.

Charles and I talked to the motel manager. He was an Asian, living with his wife and teenage son in rooms as dingy as the rest of the motel. He didn't want the young woman in his motel. For one thing, her room had been a mess to clean up that morning. And then there was the matter of payment. He assured us he was not unfeeling. But too many times he'd been tricked by promises to pay later. When I told him I was a priest, he relented and said she could stay one more night. He charged me $33 for one room, one night. Charles and I saw the room – a cramped, small space with stained, worn covering on the bed. I would have sat up all night rather than lie on that bed. Before we left I assured the weary, beaten-down little mother that we would send her help in the morning. The black couple helped her move the **three barefoot children** to the other room. **She carried all her worldly goods in three grocery bags.**

We drove back to the rectory in a kind of numb speechlessness. We were asking ourselves what is wrong with a society that produces such a family as this? What happened along the way? Who brought this little woman into the world and allowed her to receive so little education? How did things get so hopeless and bogged down?

Neither of us had answers. I could only think of our Lord's words. He said we are welcome into His kingdom if we clothe and shelter the homeless and comfort the afflicted. If we don't do these things, we are not welcome.

May God bless you all,

Fr. Dan Madigan

Dear Friends:

There is an old Irish saying **"Go often to the house of your friend for weeds choke the unused path."** In aligning yourself with our work you become not only our friend but also a member of the Food Bank family. That's why you are getting this letter. As a member of our family you are entitled to hear all the family problems.

Recently the numbers we feed have enormously multiplied. This means we reach more of the city's poor, but it also stops us from delivering the caliber of our balanced grocery bags of food which we daily dispense.

I know that many of you are already helping us with the purchase of the Arata building. Your pledges are coming in faithfully and that is so appreciated. However, because our need is so urgent and hunger hurts so much, I turn to you, my great-hearted people, as an appealing friend. I know you will help if you can.

The Good Book tells us that there is a time for everything. Now is our time to do something great.

> *"To every thing there is a season and*
> *A time to every purpose under heaven,*
> *A time to be born, and a time to die,*
> *A time to plant, and a time to pluck up that which is planted,*
> *A time to kill, and a time to heal,*
> *A time to break down, and a time to build up,*
> *A time to weep, and a time to laugh,*
> *A time to mourn, and a time to dance,*
> *A time to cast away stones, and a time to gather stones together,*
> *A time to embrace, and a time to refrain from embracing,*
> *A time to get, and a time to lose,*
> *A time to keep, and a time to cast away,*
> *A time to rend, and a time to sew,*
> *A time to keep silence, and a time to speak,*
> *A time to love, and a time to hate,*
> *A time of war, and a time of peace.*

Ecclesiastes, IV

With every good wish,

Fr. Dan Madigan

Dear Friends:

The Bible tells us that in order to get away from the crowd Jesus traveled across the lake. He had been so plagued with people. He had not even had time to eat. He was truly worn out. All day long others had been pulling at Him, demanding responses of Him.

Our volunteers often feel like that. They cannot take another interruption. They cannot deal with one more person. Jesus was tired, hungry and exhausted, and yet He felt pity toward those following Him. *"They were,"* He said, *"sheep without a shepherd."* He set His personal needs aside. With great compassion in His heart He fed all 5,000.

Sacramento Food Bank **distributes over $200,000 worth of food a month.** It takes long hours of work to convert tractor-trailer loads of loose commodities (e.g. beans, rice, powdered milk, fruits and vegetables) into small packages and then place them in the hands of hungry families. Yet, thank God, this is a daily occurrence. The people who do this need your prayers.

Yes, pray for our volunteers. Pray that they will continue to see people's pain rather than their problems. People's misery rather than their mistakes.

Please continue to support us as you have with your kind contributions. You are truly family to us. Also, please consider joining us as a volunteer if that is possible for you to do.

May the Good Lord bless each and every one of you.

Fr. Dan Madigan

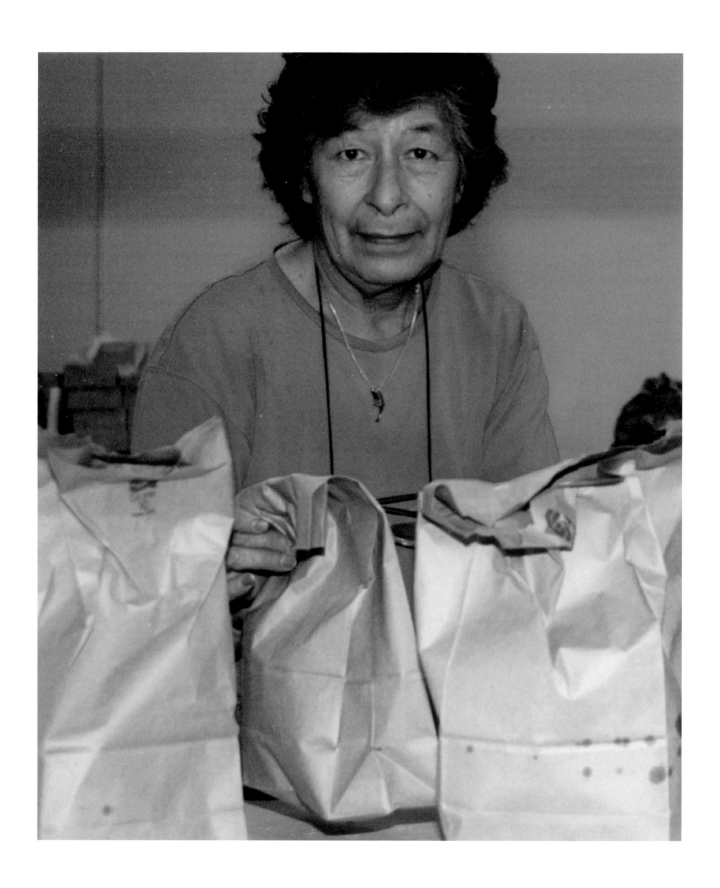

Dear Friends:

Christianity is not a one-hour-on-Sunday program. Religion cannot be separated from daily living. Neither is it something we throw on like a garment. It is inside us and it wants out. It is a genuine love of all people. It is a burning desire to rush to the hurting. It is the knowledge that we are free to fail in our efforts to help others but not free to do nothing.

Sacramento Food Bank is an **oasis of kindness.** It is responding to the problems that plague poor people. It is well acquainted with the face of the illiterate, the infant in rags, the teenager on drugs, the inhabitants of cockroach infested hovels, the unemployed with lost jobs, the empty refrigerators, the absent spouses, the alcoholic moms and the hard-working, minimum wage folks, who just cannot make enough money to support their families.

You, my friends, are in the middle of this struggle. Many of you are in the very front line – handing out the food and serving at the tables. All of you are givers – your donations keep our doors open and the food purchased, transported and distributed.

While starvation is alien to our capital city, hunger and malnutrition are not. Daily we see diets that help fill stomachs but do not properly nourish bodies. Excessive leanness and prominent abdomens are no strangers to us. This kind of plight is a brutal contradiction to our wealthy country and more especially to our Christian beliefs.

Friends – always remember no matter what your occupation is you are called to full time Christian service.

How best to respond and help the poor is up to each of us to decide. But decide we must, and act we must.

God be with you all – you are truly wonderful people.

With every good wish,

Fr. Dan Madigan

Dear Friends:

On July 18 a church janitor from Elk Grove kidnapped a young Laotian girl in the Oak Park area. The incident received wide media attention. The child's family are refugees from the Mien Hill tribe in Laos.

An article in Labor Day's newspaper claimed that most all Sacramentans are unaware of the Mien people. I find this hard to believe as Sacramento is regarded as a national mecca for this small tribe with Oak Park as their central headquarters.

Mien refugees grew up in the remote jungles of northern Laos with no schooling and with no exposure to western civilization.

Presently they are frightened and lost in our American high tech society. Their only possessions are their beautiful agrarian culture and their language which has no written form.

They were nomadic farmers in Laos. **Farming is all they know.** Presently we are trying to put together a garden for them here in Oak Park. We need your help. We have the space, the volunteers, the teachers. But we need a fence and garden tools.

If you can help us please do so. I can be reached at 456-1980 or 665-1132.

With every good wish,

Fr. Dan Madigan

Dear Friends:

I was born in rural Ireland, on Walton's mountain so to speak. All eleven of us - Mom, Dad and kids - lived in a cozy nest. We were not rich by any means but happy and secure nonetheless. Now I live in Oak Park. It is the heart of the hurting. Charles Dickens' words describe it well:

> *"It was the best of times,*
> *It was the worst of times.*
>
> *It was the age of wisdom,*
> *It was the age of foolishness.*
>
> *It was the season of light,*
> *It was the season of darkness.*
>
> *It was the spring of hope,*
> *It was the winter of despair;*
>
> *We had everything before us,*
> *We had nothing before us."*

Chaos and contradiction are rampant in our area. Oak Park has Immaculate Conception Church and the Tokyo Spa. It has McGeorge Law School and the Woodruff Hotel. It has Ellis Senior Residence and raunchy bottle shops. It has good living, breathing, feeling people and scantily-clad prostitutes. It has family stability as well as lots of alcoholic moms, absentee dads and **latchkey children.**

Here community-minded people are surrounded by the homeless, the jobless and the directionless. Streets that carry the suffering of mental illness, malnutrition and drug addition also carry the cruelty and viciousness of gangs, dope pushers and pimps. The exploited and the exploiters are on every street, however, the good far outweigh the bad. The vast majority of Oak Park residents are fine honest folk who are daily trying to make their lives work. SFBS assists many of them.

For those of you, my friends, who have not become really active with us, please do so now. Your help is badly needed. For those of you who are in the midst of the Food Bank work, please remember that our greatest glory lies not in never falling but in rising up every time we fall.

With every good wish,

Fr. Dan Madigan

Dear Friends:

People ask me why I came to California and why to Sacramento in particular. With tongue in cheek I tell them it all came about because of Hopalong Cassidy movies, which aroused in me a yearning for the open prairie. But whatever the reasons were – come I did and here I am – and now I want to express gratitude for that decision.

In this letter I wish to express my deepest thanks to:

- God, our Heavenly Father, for my years as a priest.
- The USA for graciously welcoming me some 23 years ago.
- My parishioners who have always encouraged, praised and helped me.
- The poor who have sensitized me to their world of suffering.
- And you, my friends, who join me in assisting and feeding the less fortunate.

Since childhood I have always admired the USA for its high ideals. The noble words of the Constitution, the God-like thoughts on the **Statue of Liberty** and the aspirations of so many citizens to live up to these lofty goals make this country admirable.

"Give me your tired, your poor,
Your huddled masses yearning to breathe free,
The wretched refuse of your teeming shore.
Send these, the homeless, tempest-tossed to me
I lift my lamp beside the golden door."
Emma Lazarus

"We hold these truths to be self-evident; that
all men are created equal; that they are endowed
by their Creator with certain inalienable
Rights; that among these are Life, Liberty, and
the Pursuit of Happiness."
The Declaration of Independence

A few days ago I read a letter in the Sacramento Bee with regard to the plight of the homeless. The writer said: *"Our wealth and security in this nation comes with a price tag – the necessity to give of ourselves to those less fortunate."* How true this is. This Thanksgiving Day let those of us who have a little to share give to those who have nothing.

With every good wish,

Fr. Dan Madigan

Dear Friends:

Christ did not come to the poor as a stranger, or as an outsider or as a visitor who passes by to offer sympathy and then departs.

Rather, Christ identified Himself with the poor. Like them He suffered humiliation and became Himself the victim of injustice and oppression. Bethlehem was not something that happened by chance. Nether was the Sermon on the Mount a bunch of rambling thoughts. The Cup of Cold Water was no exaggeration. Christ was totally serious when He said: *"What you do to the LEAST of My brothers, you do to Me."*

Christmas is not about neon lights, plastic reindeers and huge meals. Christmas is about Christ. It is about the Man who showed us how to live. The Man who asked us to defend His poor, protect His weak and liberate His oppressed.

On this, His Birthday, we need to truly ask ourselves – are we imitating His behavior? How are we treating His poor people? Are we helping them with their heavy load? Are we assisting them to the best of our ability? Could we give more time and support to the Food Bank, the food lockers and the soup kitchens?

Remember one of the most urgent needs among Christians today is to remove the partitions separating religion from life. We cannot go on confining religion to Sundays and to churches. We must bring the faith into everyday living. We must take religion out into the streets where the hurting is happening.

I thank you for your ongoing dedication and generosity and I wish you, all my dear friends, a very happy Christmas season.

With every good wish,

Fr. Dan Madigan

FEBRUARY 1989

Dear Friends:

In 1988 we purchased, transported, gleaned and distributed millions of pounds of food. One hundred eighty-eight thousand people came to our food outlets for help. While some of these individuals were single people, the vast majority were heads of households and carried away food not for themselves but for their families. In all, some five million meals were distributed.

For this great work I want to express my deepest gratitude to you and I want this letter to be, and only to be, a letter of sincere thanks.

Working with the poor is not at all easy. More often than not these hurting people bring with them a multitude of problems, many of which are frequently unsolvable. Over the years I have marveled at the tremendous sensitivity of all of our volunteers and notably our senior citizens. Your wisdom, perseverance and dedication serve as a headline to those of us who are trotting behind you in years.

Senior citizens – your deep concern and genuine love is also very uplifting to the unfortunate people at the other side of the window. Albert Schweitzer once said that those who have been hurt always carry the scar of that hurt with them. He claims that people who are suffering pain draw closer to others who are hurting. He calls it, *"The brotherhood of those who bear the mark of pain."* With this in mind I often think that the experience of the Great Depression was a mixed blessing as it fostered the sterling quality of charity in you.

Again to all of you, my friends, I want to say thanks once more for your goodness. Please continue the fine work which you are doing. Do not hesitate to share with me any of your ideas regarding what we should be accomplishing. Remember that the work we do is always in need of your thoughts, your prayers and your help.

With every good wish,

Fr. Dan Madigan

55

Dear Friends:

The four seasons come and the four seasons go, and each brings its own beauty and its own message. So it is with the Church's liturgical year. Advent and Christmas, Lent and Easter, all highlight different aspects of our religious life.

This Lenten season was a very special one for me. I saw fasting in a different way than ever before. It was the prophet Isaiah that set me straight. Let me share with you his words:

> *"Is this the manner of fasting I wish,*
> *of keeping a day of penance:*
> *That a man bow his head like a reed,*
> *And lie in sackcloth and ashes?*
> *Do you call this a fast, a day acceptable to the LORD?*
> *This, rather, is the fasting that I wish:*
> *releasing those bound unjustly,*
> *untying the thongs of the yoke;*
> *setting free the oppressed, breaking every yoke;*
> *sharing your bread with the hungry,*
> *sheltering the oppressed and the homeless:*
> *Clothing the naked when you see them,*
> *And not turning your back on your own."*

Now the Easter season is upon us and what message does it bring? **Easter is an everlasting sign of life.** It tells us that sin, evil and death can be overcome with holiness and resurrection. It shows us –

- that hope overcomes despair
- that truth is stronger than falsehood
- that justice sweeps away injustice
- that freedom destroys slavery
- that peace casts aside crime and violence
- that above all else, life lasts forever

Yes, my friends, Easter is indeed here. Death is no more. Heaven is ours. Let us rejoice and thank God for our wonderful beliefs and the beautiful people we see every day.

May the Risen Christ bless you all,

Fr. Dan Madigan

Dear Friends:

Poverty is on the increase nationwide. Locally it's booming, according to our own food locker figures. In 1976, 2,700 people came to us seeking food. In 1988, 140,809 people came to us with the same need.

My 13 year journey ('76-'89) from Immaculate Conception's church basement to Arata Center has taught me a great deal about food, administration, volunteers, fundraising, computers, refrigeration, trucks, vans, trailers and forklifts. I have also learned about human failure, power failure and food spoilage, but above all, the years have taught me how complex the nature of poverty is.

Poverty stretches all the way from mere shortage to total destitution. The same is true of the people who come to us for help. It is a mistake to classify the disadvantaged. To assume that they are cheaters, loafers and chiselers is an outrage. A diversity of people of all ages, creeds and colors come to our food outlets. Derelicts, winos and street people stand in the long lines with the mentally ill, the drug addicts, the prostitutes. We see the totally unskilled, the illiterate, the unemployable, the physically handicapped, the chronically ill, the socially stunted, and the elderly.

The frightening fact is this: The majority of those who come to us look and act like ourselves. They are local, neighborhood folk – moms and dads who have run out of money because their meager income, be it welfare or minimum wage, is not enough to live on. Only a mellow and flexible person is able to work at the distribution window and successfully interact with the many different individuals. A high level of charity, kindness and patience is imperative for the job, as volunteers quickly learn. After all, clients bring their personalities as well as their problems to the window. Some are crude. Some are hostile. Some try to lie and cheat. But the vast majority is very kind, receptive and extremely grateful for the help they are receiving.

Daily the poor come for help. So, thank God, does the food. Every month $200,000 worth of food comes into and goes out from our warehouse. It comes to us via our own direct purchasing, Senior Gleaners, Inc., government commodities, factory, store and food outlets, churches, schools and clubs, fraternities and neighborhood food drives, and many, many private donations. From the warehouse this food is transported to our food lockers and soup kitchens where it is broken down, packaged and distributed directly to people in need.

Daily I ask myself if I should be **'showing people how to fish"** rather than giving them "a fish." Is it more Christian to attack the sources of suffering instead of relieving that suffering? Is concern for social change more Christ-like than compassionate help for immediate need? Both are important, but we cannot do everything. So we do what we can. Because of you I feel we have climbed two mountains of need. With you, our donors and volunteers, we now feed and clothe the poor and we do it well. Our 12,000 square-foot clothing outlet is the result of years of experimentation. It now runs smoothly, benefiting families and singles alike. But there are more mountains to conquer. These we are eyeing in the hope of successfully taking on their challenges, with the good Lord's never-failing help.

Above all, we ask for your prayers, that God will show us clearly what needs to be done and inspire us with the way to go about it.

With every good wish,

Fr. Dan Madigan

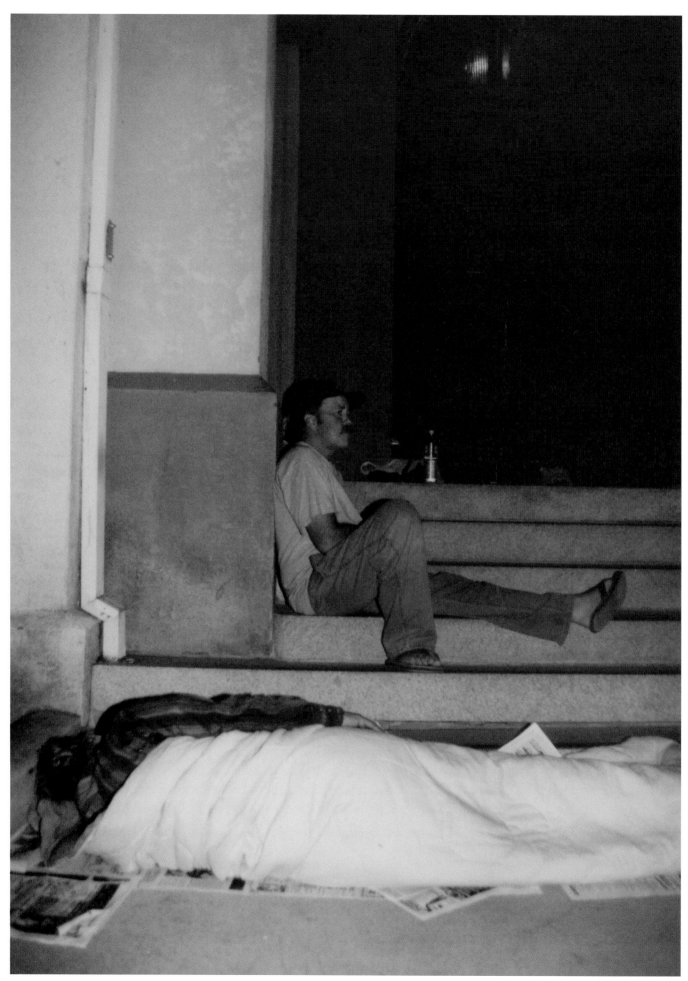

Dear Friends:

The food locker windows have shown me poverty, and the soup kitchen tables have certainly added their share. But it is the nighttime rectory door knocks that have exposed me to the fear and stress of the homeless family.

The late evenings of the Del Paso Heights '60's brought families to our door. They came for a religious blessing. They came for some consolation. They came because one of them was leaving the next morning for Vietnam.

Nighttime still brings weatherbeaten families to our rectory door here in Oak Park. They come now because of today's war – the war of having **nowhere to lay their heads.**

These unwanted and isolated parents are afraid to take their children to the homeless shelter. The angry outbursts, explosive behaviors and cultural clashes that they know or think exist there frightens them. They willingly accept sleeping mats on our open porch. They are even pleased to bed down in the newspaper collection truck as it offers them the privacy, safety and quietness they long for so much.

Derelicts, drifters and hoboes are not the only homeless people in California. Half of the Golden State's 2.3 million hungry are children, and so are one-third of its 150,000 homeless.

Having no home disintegrates a family. It wears away morale and self-esteem. It has disastrous effects on physical health. The hardship of having to rough it in conditions of poor nutrition and squalor takes its toll. Children begin to exhibit aggressive behavior, hyperactivity and signs of depression. Adults come up with diseases such as chronic bronchitis, emphysema and tuberculosis.

My friends, as God loving people we cannot stand by and ignore this situation. It's not right we do so. We have to help put together an atmosphere of warmth, affection and affirmation for these wounded families. Please join me.

May God bless you for what you are already doing for the poor of Sacramento.

With every good wish,

Fr. Dan Madigan

Dear Friends:

My introduction to the USA was assignment in the Del Paso Heights of the 60's. Poverty and racial unrest were there but so was law and order. Police seemed in control and motorists stopped at pedestrian crossings. Today, after having picked up broken bodies on a Broadway crosswalk, and having seen a ricocheting bullet in my church office and having worked with victims of every imaginable crime, I realize how much times have changed.

Living in Del Paso Heights and Oak Park has shown me that interaction between affluent neighborhoods and inner-city streets does not exist. Economics sees to that. However, thanks to my profession I move on both sides of that fence. I see strong families with career aspirations as well as grade school dropouts from crime-infested streets.

Constantly I ask what future have people with zero skills, zero work habits, zero moral values and zero aspirations. Is it idleness, illiteracy, irresponsibility, illegitimacy, that causes urban blight? Is it alcoholism, drug abuse, criminality and violence that lead to this destitution? Are burglaries, muggings and rape, the chicken or the egg? Is the lack of money the sole cause of poverty? Could a change in economics set everything right?

We all know that without its banks a stream becomes a swamp. The river banks of the Great Depression were repaired because people had the equipment to do the job. Family togetherness, accountability, determination, courage and self-esteem. These values have to come back. There is no other answer.

Sacramento made Humphrey the Whale a celebrity. Sacramento is now hounding the homeless from these same river banks. These broken families need more than a homeless shelter or a food locker or a counseling center. They need mentors. They need kind and charitable common sense people who are prepared to lead them from where they are to where they should be.

To do this mentors will need very specific training. They will need immediate and ongoing access to an organization that will provide them with the tools to do the job. For their homeless families, mentors will need housing, food, clothing, baby supplies, schools for children, adult education for parents, job counseling, household furniture, bedding and appliances. The mentors themselves will also need much support and supervision. This is something I feel we can provide to them.

To sum up, the Sacramento Food Bank is striving to be the needed agency that I have just outlined. For 14 years I have worked with you at putting this package of care together. I feel **we are still on the mountainside but very near the top. Please help us to get to the summit.**

With every good wish,

Fr. Dan Madigan

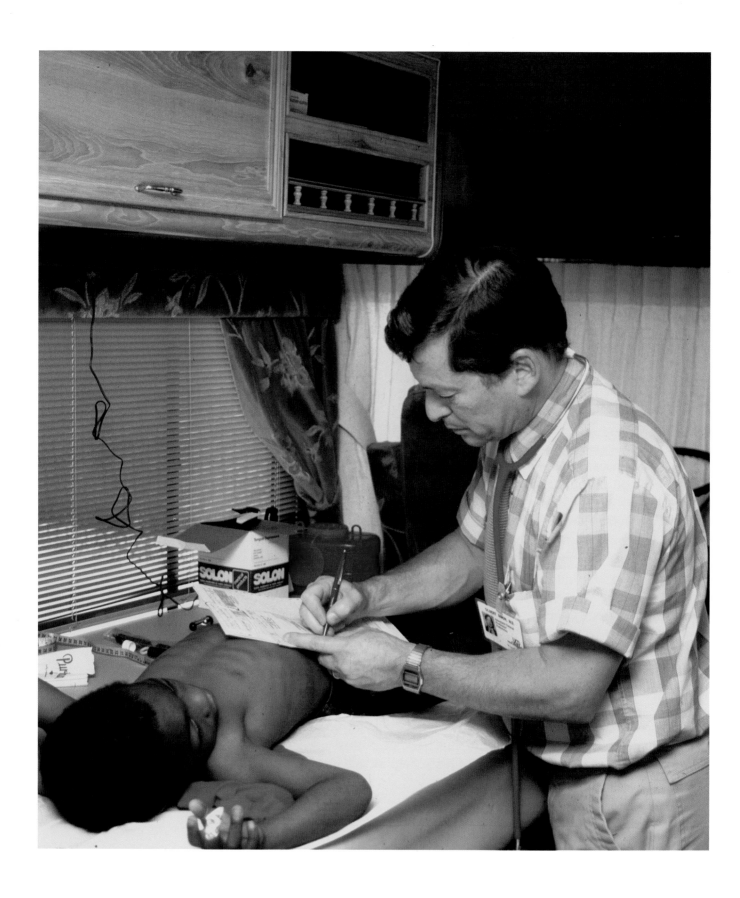

SEPTEMBER 1989

Dear Friends:

Thanks to my recent appointment as pastor of St. Joseph's Church in Clarksburg, I am now smelling the roses, walking the dogs, and enjoying my evenings on the banks of the Sacramento River.

Fourteen years at Immaculate Conception parish were wonderful and hectic. I left there with scores of beautiful memories and lots of true friends. May God bless you, I. C. Church. I will never forget you.

Our Food Bank is going very well. We will distribute $3,000,000 worth of food this year. One hundred forty-five thousand people will come in person to our distribution windows and will take home food to their families. Twenty thousand people will come for clothing, and forty thousand people will sit at our table for Sunday afternoon meals.

While all this is going on, 50 or so adult students will be meeting with their teachers on a one-to-one basis. Their aim is to improve their literacy skills. At the same time **pediatrician Dr. Gil Simon will be seeing hundreds of infants and young people in his mobile unit** in our parking lot.

This God-given work is happening because of you. Eight-hundred and twenty of you are volunteers and have hands-on information on what I am talking about. The rest of you are well acquainted with our work because of your financial contributions and commitments. All of you are essential to the operation. You are the lifeblood of the work that is happening here. Without you we would not exist.

Am I financially strapped or am I financially okay? To answer this question I would like to say that I am extremely grateful to God for the contributions that keep coming in. Together with my staff I try to stretch and manage your money to the very best of my ability. We are in debt, but I have spent most of my life in that position. We are struggling but, Thank God, we are not drowning. I guess what I am saying is that we need you very badly, otherwise we cannot keep going.

In my last newsletter I mentioned doing something in regard to housing for the poor. Approximately 50 people expressed an interest in working with us. My Thanksgiving newsletter will carry more details on this.

In the meantime, may God bless you all for your kindness and generosity. You are beautiful and wonderful people. If there is anything I can do for you, or if there is any specific request that you would like to make of me, please do not hesitate to give me a call here at the Food Bank.

With every good wish,

Fr. Dan Madigan

Dear Friends:

A few days after the big quake some of us from the Sacramento Food Bank went to Watsonville. We took ten tons of food along. We came away different people, and we swore we would go back with more help.

St. Patrick's Church and rectory looked like a bombed-out war zone. Much of its school was damaged. In its auditorium the neighborhood people were feeding and consoling one another.

We walked around the town. Two hundred families were on the streets. Their houses were no longer available to them. The city signs were posted on their doors *"Danger – Do Not Enter – Not Safe to Occupy."*

These few lines describe what we saw:

> *"Watsonville town is hurting bad*
> *low moans and prayers resound*
> *each family has its tale of woe*
> *and fear is hovering round.*
> *To and fro the volunteers move*
> *the touch of their hands*
> *a smile, a whisper or a prayer*
> *makes each sad heart expand."*

Many, many thanks to **all you wonderful people who brought by 3,500 pounds of food,** 300 blankets and generous money donations on the night before we went to Watsonville. Bishop Quinn, thank you for being with us in the loading of the truck. You gave us all the inspiration we needed. Friends – let's never forget the message of our Blessed Lord:

> *"Where pain dwells with poverty*
> *and the way is dark and cold*
> *they that make the path more bright*
> *shall reap a hundredfold."*

May God bless you for all your kindness to the hurting people of Watsonville.

With every good wish,

Fr. Dan Madigan

Dear Friends:

Jesus Christ practiced and preached volunteerism. He repeatedly said He came to serve not to be served. He asked His followers to feed the hungry, clothe the naked, shelter the homeless and take care of the little children.

I believe that the law of life is that nothing can come into us unless it can get out of us.

We commonly think that study is the road to learning, but continued study alone will eventually only paralyze a mind. The person who really wishes to learn must not only study but also apply the knowledge gained to practical uses. Somehow one must give back what one gets or one will lose what one gets.

The Dead Sea has an inlet but no outlet. Its water level is maintained by evaporation. I believe that's what also happens to knowledge that is not used. It evaporates.

Electricity, on the other hand, has an inlet and an outlet. Power runs through its wire, and so it must be with us. God's love is meant to travel through us to others.

We just cannot become a Dead Sea. We cannot stagnate. Lots of work needs to be done.

Please give me a call. Step forward, volunteer and join our team.

With every good wish to you and yours,

Fr. Dan Madigan

Dear Friends:

Fiorello LaGuardia, mayor of New York City during the worst days of the Depression, was a lovable, eccentric, egotistical, fearless friend of the people. He did some crazy things. He used to ride on a fire truck to be there with people during fire emergencies. He took whole orphanages to baseball games, and when the New York newspapers went on strike, he read the comics to the people over the radio.

One cold winter night in 1935 he showed up at night court and asked the judge to let him take over for the evening. He hadn't been at it long when a poor woman came before him accused of stealing food.

"What's this all about?" LaGuardia asked. The woman explained that her daughter's husband had abandoned her, and her daughter was sick and had no money for food. She had taken the food in order to feed her sick daughter and nurse her back to health.

Then the shopkeeper, from whom the food was stolen, had his chance to speak. *"It's a bad neighborhood, your honor. There has to be some punishment so that everybody who is in need doesn't go stealing. You have to teach a lesson not to steal, your honor."*

LaGuardia answered, *"You're right."* Then to the woman he said, *"I have to punish you. The law does not make exceptions. Ten dollars or ten days in jail."* And as he said those words he took from his wallet a $10 bill and put it in his large hat. *"Here's the $10 fine – and I further fine everyone in this courtroom 50 cents for living in a city where people have to steal food in order to eat."* He passed his hat around. The bailiff collected 50 cents from all present – including the store owner, attorneys, petty criminals, traffic violators and City cops.

All told $47.50 was collected and handed to the woman.

Sacramentans, I am not a judge and I am certainly not your mayor, but I am in a position to say that our beautiful city has some very hungry people. Because of this hunger, we all need to be fined.

I will start like LaGuardia did by fining myself. Please join me – fine yourself whatever you should and send in your fine.

May God bless all for your wonderful kindness,

Fr. Dan Madigan

Dear Friends:

Living in Clarksburg, below the river banks, has taught me the value of the levee. Without that river levee our church and grounds would become a swamp.

The people of the Great Depression never lost their river banks. Family togetherness, accountability, determination, courage and self-esteem never left them. Today it's different. Our societal river banks are burst. They have to be repaired.

Broken people and shattered families need more than a homeless shelter or a food locker or a soup kitchen. They need common sense people who can lead them from where they are to where they should be. **They need dedicated folks who will walk with them, step by step, as they journey from destitution to self-actualization.**

Please continue to be a part of us. We are putting a great package of care together. We need your involvement. The following poems will help you with ongoing soul searching:

AM I A FORGIVING PERSON?

There's a wideness in God's mercy
Like the wideness of the sea;
There's a kindness in His justice,
Which is more than liberty.
There is welcome for the sinner,
And more graces for the good;
There is mercy with the Savior;
There is healing in His blood.

There is no place where earth's sorrows
Are more felt than up in heaven;
There is no place where earth's failings
Have such kindly judgment given.
There is plentiful redemption
In the blood that has been shed;
There is joy for all the members
In the sorrows of the Head.

For the love of God is broader
Than the measure of man's mind;
And the heart of the Eternal
Is most wonderfully kind
If our love were but more simple,
We should take him at His word;
And our lives would be all sunshine
In the sweetness of the Lord.
                    Ian D. Mitchell

AM I JUDGMENTAL?

When some fellow yields to temptation
And breaks a conventional law
We look for no good in his make-up
But God! How we look for a flaw!
No one will ask, "How tempted?"
Nor allow for the battles he's fought
His name becomes food for the jackals
For us who have never been caught.

"He has sinned!" we shout from the housetops
We forget the good he has done
We center on one lost battle
And forget the times he has won.
"Come! Gaze on the sinner!" We thunder
"And by his example be taught
That his footsteps lead to destruction"
Cry we who have never been caught.

I'm a sinner, O Lord, and I know it
I'm weak, I blunder, I fail
I'm tossed on life's stormy ocean
Like ships embroiled in a gale
I'm willing to trust in Thy mercy
To keep the commandments Thou'st taught
But deliver me, Lord, from the judgment
Of saints who have never been caught.
                    Francis Keenan, C.P.

May God bless you all and grant you a very happy Easter.

With every good wish,

Fr. Dan.

Fr. Dan Madigan

Dear Friends:

Poverty is escalating daily. What, you may ask, is needed to right this terrible situation. Well, it's certainly not more studies, surveys, polls, or commissions as the following words of wisdom clearly state:

I was hungry,
and you formed a humanities club and discussed my hunger.
I was imprisoned,
and you crept off quietly to your chapel in the cellar and prayed for my release.
I was naked,
and in your mind you debated the morality of my appearance.
I was sick,
and you knelt and thanked God for your health.
I was homeless,
and you preached to me the spiritual shelter of the love of God.
I was lonely,
and you left me alone to pray for me.
You seem so holy, so close to God,
But, I'm still very hungry, And lonely, And cold.

Yes, action on all our parts is truly needed. We can do something as Edward Everett Hale clearly lets us know:

"I am only one,
But still, I am one.
I can do something,
And because I cannot do everything,
I will not refuse to do something that I can do."

Please do think and pray about joining us. We need your help very much.

With every good wish,

FR. DAN.

Fr. Dan Madigan

Dear Friends:

Reverend Mother Bridget O'Shaughnessy had a policy for her Sacramento-based convent that all beggars coming to their door would receive a dollar.

She felt that any one of these hurting people might very well be St. Peter in disguise. Her wisdom was questioned one day by a young novice who claimed that the man at the door was very drunk, could not possibly be St. Peter and was not deserving of help. Reverend Mother's response was *"**Sister, give the man the dollar** – he may very well be St. Patrick."*

At our food outlets we see them all – St. Patricks and St. Peters. Some have caused their own misfortunes. The majority have not. These are victims of multitudinous problems – physical handicaps, mental illness, broken homes, minimum wages.

Our volunteers are truly wonderful. Daily they hear all about hunger, homelessness and empty refrigerators. Daily they see excessive leanness and prominent abdomens. Daily their desire is to ease the pain and hurt that seems ever present.

You, my friends, make up the rest of the team. Through your generous donations you are keeping the ship afloat. We are your novices answering the door. You are the generous Mother Superior showing us the way.

My fellow pilgrims, may the blessings promised to the compassionate be yours in abundance.

With much love and every blessing,

Fr. Dan Madigan

Dear Friends:

It's heartwarming to see people travel from poverty to prosperity. It's sad to see people slide from comfort to destitution. The Talmud puts it well, ***"Life is a wheel – he who is on top today may be on the bottom tomorrow."***

Ronald Reagan's great-grandfather was born in Ireland in a bogland area called Doolis, near the town of Ballyporeen, in the County of Tipperary. Here is a journalist's description of a visit paid in those days to the Reagan ancestral neighborhood.

> *"A starved-looking and half-naked old woman, barefooted and shivering with
> age and pain, besought me to see her cabin in Doolis. The unfortunate creature had built it herself
> of sod and stones, and thatched it with heather and rushes.
> The approaches to it were swimming with liquid manure and mud; the odors around the place were
> revolting. A course platter of yellow stirabout without even salt represented the whole food of the
> establishment and an iron pot the entire furniture."*

It's no wonder that the Reagan family left there. Ireland with its hunger, turmoil and oppression was too cruel for them. The New World with its freedom, hope and opportunity turned their wheel of life around.

My family, my teachers, my parishoners and the good folks of Sacramento all helped in turning my wheel of life to where it is today. I hope I will never forget that. I hope too that I will never lose sight of Shakespeare's advice *"not to scorn the steps by which we ascend the ladder of life."*

Because of your supportive empathy we do help people turn their wheel of life around. We feed them, we clothe them, we befriend them, we educate them. We let them know they are beautiful and important. Thank you for your wonderful kindness to the poor. May God truly bless you for your kind heart.

With every good wish,

Fr. Dan Madigan

The Sacramento Bee

Editorial - The Sacramento Bee Sunday October 21, 1991

OPINION

Homeless Havens

With the crisis in the gulf, this budget mess in Washington and upcoming elections, the homeless have slipped off the front pages of most newspapers. But they are still out there, an estimated 9,000 in Sacramento County alone, and still in need of help.

Homeless Havens, a privately funded charity organized by the Rev. Dan Madigan of Sacramento, provides homeless families with a place to live and guidance on how to live. It consists of a collection of renovated houses, nine so far. The formerly homeless families pay no rent for a year. During that time they are matched with mentor couples, volunteers who will help them re-enter mainstream society.

The theory behind this program is that the poor often need more than shelter. They may need at least a year's worth of attention - someone to teach them how to find and hold a job, pay their bills, keep their children in school and save a little money. That's the mentor's job - part practical advice and part moral support. Initially, mentors meet with the formerly homeless family twice a week or more to help them get settled and set goals. Mentors must be happy and productive in their own lives and prepared to accept the harsh reality in which some families live.

For so many who live in comfort and are haunted by the thought of hungry children sleeping in cars and parks and under bridges, Homeless Havens provides a very concrete way to help. Over the year the program's been in existence, six couples have been recruited as mentors. Organizers hope to increase that to 20 or more. That kind of expansion will require more houses, money and volunteers. The person to contact is Madigan, at 456-1980.

The Sacramento Bee

Locally owned and edited for 133 years
James McClatchy, editor, 1857 - 1883

C.K. McClatchy, editor, president, 1883 - 1936
Walter P. Jones, editor 1936 - 1974

Eleanor McClatchy, president, 1936 - 1978
C.K. McClatchy, editor, 1974 - 1989

Gregory E. Favre, executive editor

Peter Schrag, editorial page editor

Frank R.J. Whittaker, president and general manager

Compiled by Fr. Dan Madigan, printed in-house at the SFBS print shop

Dear Friends:

One out of every four children in Sacramento County lives in a welfare family. Often hungry these children live in poverty. They are sometimes homeless. I work with them and have for the past 25 years.

Having no home disintegrates a family. Loss of a home wears away their morale and self-esteem. It has disastrous effects on their physical and mental health.

Homeless families need more than a *"shelter"* or a *"warehouse"* or an *"army barracks."* **They need a real home,** a place of privacy and security where they can rest and rekindle themselves. They also need a mentor. Mentors are specially trained people who have the dedication, skill and tools to lead families from where they are right now to where they should and can be at a later date.

The putting together of this package of care is something we have been working on for some time. The Homeless Havens Board has drawn up the blueprints of how we will do our job. Dear friends of ours have donated nine homes. We have hired a full-time program director. The flag is up and we are ready to sail.

Yes, more houses will be procured. Mentors will be trained. Families will be put back on their feet. Old values will return. Self-esteem will be instilled. Charitable, caring conduct will be established as the daily norm.

You, my friends, are in no way off the hook. Think about this letter. Pray about it. Decide how you are going to help. Then give me a call.

How about motivating your organizations, your churches, your businesses or perhaps your friends to contribute a house to our homeless program? Houses can be donated as outright gifts or loaned for a specified time limit.

With every good wish,

Fr. Dan Madigan

Dear Friends:

Every year the federal government prints office calendars for the upcoming year. In 1972 somebody in government made a colossal mistake about the calendar. It designated the wrong day for the **Thanksgiving holiday.**

Rather than destroy over one billion calendars, the General Service Administration decided to simply attach a correction to each of them and let it go at that. It was a very practical decision, but the correction they attached spoke volumes! It read:

"Please excuse, but we're giving thanks on the wrong day this year.
It should be November 22nd."

Thanksgiving is not just a day on the calendar. Neither has it to do with the abundance of our possessions. It has to do with our heart. Embracing – God as our Father – all people as family – and hurting folks as the sisters, brothers and children we willingly help.

With this in mind let us pray:

> *Thank you our Father for so many things,*
> *Thanks for the Joy that Thanksgiving brings.*
>
> *Thanks for the Stars in the Heaven above,*
> *Thanks for the freedom in this land we love.*
>
> *Thanks for the Sun and the gentle breeze,*
> *The patter of rain the rustle of leaves.*
>
> *Thanks for the mountains the air so pure,*
> *For the Strength and Courage of hard trails to endure.*
>
> *Thanks for the trees that stand so tall,*
> *Put there by You for one and for all.*
>
> *Thanks for the beauty that Nature unfolds,*
> *The Faith of loved ones to have and to hold.*
>
> *Thank You our Father for SO many things,*
> *Thanks for the Joy that Thanksgiving brings.*

May God truly bless you all. And may your kind hearts continue to grow.

With every good wish,

Fr. Dan Madigan

Dear Friends:

When I came to the Food Bank yesterday the Sunday afternoon lunch was well under way.

Being the fourth Sunday of the month, all the familiar faces from Our Lady of Assumption Church in Carmichael were present. Everything was going well. It was a beehive of activity.

After a meeting in my office I found that the warehouse had quieted down. Doors were closed. The majority of the volunteers had left. Ed DeWinter, Mario Stefani, Joe Ostoja, Floyd Ahern, Dan Rife, all who come every Sunday and most who have come since we began the program in March 1983, were doing the final wrap-up. The meat slicer was taken apart. Dishes were washed. Mario handed me a little piece of paper saying they had just served 865 people.

As I walked out of the warehouse, I saw hungry faces at the fence. Six or eight people, very frustrated, very hungry and very much in need had come too late. The doors were closed. I told them I would see what I could do for them.

The Bible tells us that in order to get away from the crowds, Jesus traveled across the lake. He had been so plagued with people that He had not even had time to eat. He needed time alone. He was truly worn out. All day long others had been pulling at Him, demanding responses.

Yesterday when I returned to the warehouse I found that our volunteers felt like Jesus. They couldn't take another interruption. They couldn't deal with any more people. They were tired and exhausted, yet like Christ, their kind hearts took control. They scurried around the warehouse once more. **They fed those extra folks at the gate.**

Friends, please pray for our volunteers. Pray for my staff. Pray for me. Pray that our eyes will continue to see the pain rather than the problem, the misery rather than the mistakes. Also, please continue to support us as you have. You are truly our family.

May the Good Lord bless each and every one of you.

With every good wish,

Fr. Dan Madigan

Dear Friends:

Today a great cloud of sorrow lies over the Food Bank.

Staff member **Chuck Withrow, one of the dearest and sweetest of people,** died after a very short illness. We are all in shock. Despite our belief that this wonderful man is in the company of Almighty God, we nevertheless miss him greatly.

On Saturday I will have the privilege of officiating at his Mass of Burial at St. Joseph's Church in Modesto. The Gospel I will use will be from Matthew 25:31-40:

> *"When the Son of Man comes in His glory, escorted by all the angels of heaven, He will sit upon His royal throne, and all the nations will be assembled before Him. Then He will separate them into groups, as a shepherd separates sheep from goats. The sheep He will place on His right hand, the goats on His left. The king will say to those on His right: Come. You have my Father's blessing! Inherit the kingdom prepared for you from the creation of the world. For I was hungry and you gave me food, I was thirsty and you gave me drink. I was a stranger and you welcomed me, naked and you clothed me. I was ill and you comforted me, in prison and you came to visit me.*
>
> *Then the just will ask Him: Lord, when did we see you hungry and feed you or see you thirsty and give you drink? When did we welcome you away from home or clothe you in your nakedness? When did we visit you when you were ill or in prison?*
>
> *The king will answer them: I assure you, as often as you did it for one of my least brothers, you did it for me."*

With these above words in mind, can you imagine the reception Chuck received when he entered the Gates of Heaven? I even suspect that by this time he has shared with the Good Lord some of his hearty jokes and probably has played a few rounds of golf with the Saints.

Friends, the numbers at our food outlets have increased by 35% since one year ago. Moneywise we are falling very short. Please see what you can do for us.

I wish you all a very Happy Easter season.

With every good wish,

Fr. Dan Madigan

Dear Friends:

History has been hard on dreamers like Gandhi, Kennedy, King and Christ. All paid a big price for their dreams. Miles Connelly, in his book "Mr. Blue," warns us to be careful when wandering into the dreaming field. He says:

> *"Conservative historians describe any man with a passion for greatness as a megalomaniac. Conservative citizens regard such a man with suspicion. 'Look at him, they say to one another, the idiot! Why doesn't he settle down and establish himself in the community? Why is he forever restless, forever trying to get something beyond himself? The man is crazy.'"*

Who wants to be classified as crazy? What church community is willing to wear that badge? It's no small wonder that, as individuals or as a parish we pick the easy way out and **walk the middle of the road.** Yet walking that safe, middle of the road route has its downfalls as Miles Connelly points out:

> *"These conservatives are partly right. Play your life safe, and you'll never die on St. Helena. Your failure is measured by your aspirations. Aspire not, and you cannot fail. Columbus died in chains, Joan of Arc was burned at the stake. Let us all live snugly – and life will soon be little more than a thick, gelatinous stream of comfortability and ignorance."*

Becoming a thick, gelatinous stream of comfortability and ignorance is a big price to pay for turning in on one's self. It's the cost we endure when refusing to carry out the corporal works of mercy: of uplifting the downtrodden, feeding the hungry, clothing the naked, sheltering the homeless and educating the ignorant. After all, bettering and brightening the lives of the unfortunate is our true mission in life. Refusing to take part means being less Christian while jumping in automatically entails joining the ranks of those great dreamers who have paved the way ahead of us.

God bless – take care of yourselves.

With every good wish,

Fr. Dan Madigan

94

Dear Friends:

Ireland's eighteenth century poet, Thomas Moore, wrote the following lines:

> *"Oft in the stilly night,*
> *Ere slumber's chain has bound me,*
> *Fond memory brings the light*
> *Of other days around me."*

Many a night before going to sleep my mind journeys to bygone days, past events and different places.

Recently it journeyed to my hometown and in its wanderings I found the answer to a problem we were having at the Food Bank. Let me explain.

Limerick is my home city in Ireland. We have Franciscan fathers there. As a child, I was always told that if the Friary ever ran short of food it would ring its church bells.

Some years ago this happened. **The bells rang out** at an unusual hour. The fathers needed help. Limerick City residents responded very, very generously.

Like the Limerick Franciscans we recently had to ring our bells, so to speak. Our volunteers called many of you on the phone for immediate help. Your response was truly great.

Times are tough. Daily more and more families are showing up at our distribution windows. In fact, the numbers we serve have doubled since last year. Unemployment is rampant. This was brought home to me in the past few weeks when I advertised in the local newspaper for an administrative secretary. One hundred forty-seven responded. Most were very qualified.

I sincerely apologize for the frequency of requests for help. But I have no choice. The need is great. We just cannot turn our back on the poor and walk away.

May God truly bless you for your ongoing support of our Food Bank.

With every good wish,

Fr. Dan Madigan

Dear Friends:

Today our societal priorities seem completely out of whack. I feel that if you meditate on the following facts for a while you will agree with me.

- **Movies cost many millions to produce**

- The average major league baseball player's salary is $900,000 annually

- Boxers are given as high as $30 million to step into the ring

- Our country is Four Trillion dollars in debt

- One out of every five of our children grows up in poverty

- 25 percent of our teenagers drop out of school

- 10 million U.S. people live on the edge of homelessness

- 37 million families have no medical insurance

Yes indeed, it's because our priorities are all topsy-turvy that our great nation is now producing two distinct countries: one that is working and productive and one that is depressed and hopeless.

So, my friends, the days are long gone when we can afford to be passive recipients of what's going on around us. We have to stand up and say our piece and say it loudly. Ignoring issues is not the way to live.

With every good wish,

Fr. Dan Madigan

Dear Friends:

Many years of inner city living have shown me lots of misery. Poverty, hunger and deprivation. Filth, disease and mental illness, illiteracy, unemployment and latchkey kids.

Dysfunctional people, incapacitated families and the deinstitutionalized mentally ill have been with SFBS from the beginning. They still are. But now they have new companions.

Today's food line is mostly made up of hard-working, low-paid family people, fixed income elderly and the neatly dressed and highly embarrassed unemployed. All have the same to say. That no matter how they stretch their income it will not cover rent, utilities, medical care, clothing and food for their family.

Our police chief is amazed at what's happening. His statistics show that when the first six months of 1991 are compared with those for 1990 there is an increase in armed robbery of 32 percent. I am also flabbergasted to see that when we make that same comparison at our Sacramento Food Bank operation, we run into a 50 percent increase in numbers.

So gone are the days for mere social interest and community concern. Immediate action is needed. The galling chains of poverty and illiteracy that so often shackle people to crime and even push them into gangs and narcotics need to be broken.

These people need mentors. Mentors show hurting families that an alternative lifestyle is within their reach. **Mentors work with them on their journey of change.** Mentors help them develop the physical, emotional and intellectual powers to make this journey. Mentoring works. It has for us.

Please continue to support us as you have. If you need to talk to me about any ideas you have or additional commitment you want to make, do give me a call at (916) 456-1980.

May our good God truly bless you.

With every good wish,

Fr. Dan Madigan

Dear Friends:

Charity is not just something we throw on like a garment. Goodness is inside us and it wants out. It is a genuine love of all people. It is a burning desire to rush to the hurting. It is the knowledge that we are free to fail in our effort to help others, but not free to do nothing.

Sacramento Food Bank is an oasis of kindness. It responds to the problems that plague poor people. It is well acquainted with the illiterate face, the hungry child, the frightened unemployed. It knows all about hard-working, minimum wage folk who just cannot make enough on which to live.

Our volunteers are in the middle of this struggle. Daily they are in the very front line. Daily they hand out food and hand out encouragement.

Now, while starvation is alien to our Capital City, hunger and malnutrition are not. Daily we see empty stomachs and poorly nourished bodies. Their existence is a brutal contradiction to our wealthy country and to our God-given beliefs.

Friends, always remember no matter what our occupation is, we are called to full-time, God-given service. How best to respond is up to each of us, but decide we must. Act we must.

May God be with you this Thanksgiving season. You are truly wonderful people.

With every good wish,

Fr. Dan Madigan

Dear Friends:

Even though I've been in this world for quite a few years, I still have very fond and vivid memories of the Christmas seasons of my youth.

Christmas then was very much a season. It began with Christmas Eve Mass (*Big Christmas)* and ended with the Feast of the Epiphany, Jan. 6 (*Little Christmas).*

Walking with the adults to Christmas Eve Mass, enjoying the privilege of staying up late, admiring the moonlit night, and feeling warm and cozy in my new sweater, new overcoat and new Wellingtons (rubber boots), which Santa had just delivered, are all experiences that I will never forget.

My mother was a very practical Santa Claus. She explained to us children that Santa was a wise person, who knew exactly what gifts we needed, and that's what we got.

Mom and Dad reared us well. They taught us love of God and love of neighbor. They told us that life was a hill that had to be climbed and they helped us acquire the discipline needed to do the job.

Today I live in the Delta, three quarters of a million acres of flatland, one thousand miles of waterways, fifty-five man-made islands, seventy bridges, and lots of meandering embankments.

Drainage levees and sloughs turned this onetime wild marsh into what it is today, the producer of fruits, vegetables, corn, grapes and grasses. In other words, discipline did the job.

Here at the Food Bank we feed, house, clothe and educate people. And we do more than that. We help people travel from where they are now to where they should be. This journey calls for:

- knowledge on our part (*a plan)*
- guides to lead people along (*mentors)*
- and, a wanting on the part of recipients (*discipline)*

You are the people that make all of this possible. You all help in different ways. God bless you for your generosity.

May the good Lord shower on you His abundant blessings during this Christmas season.

With every good wish,

Fr. Dan Madigan

Dear Friends:

St. Patrick's Day is almost upon us and we Irish celebrate it with great gusto. We Irish in America feel we have so much to be grateful for including religious freedom, political freedom and bread on our tables.

For us Irish people hunger means:

- The Great Hunger. The Irish potato famine of 1846 and 1847.

- Starvation, destitution, evictions and shallow graves.

- Two million people dying in the hovels, roads and ditches of Ireland.

- Millions boarding "coffin ships" for the United States of America.

- Dying by thousands crossing the Atlantic Ocean.

- Entering the USA and becoming children of the slums.

- At the same time because of British control of our country, shiploads of wheat, oats

  and flour were leaving the Irish ports for foreign destinations.

Hunger was a good teacher. It produced great sensitivity in the hearts of many people. It prompted an Irishman to write these lines:

> *"Where sickness dwells with poverty*
> *and the way is dark and cold*
> *they that made the path more bright*
> *shall reap a hundred-fold."*

I have always claimed that generosity to the poor brings its own reward. Recently I heard a story that verifies this very well. Dr. Karl Menninger, the famous psychiatrist, once gave a lecture on mental health and afterward answered questions from the audience. *"What would you advise a person to do"* asked one man, *"if that person felt a nervous breakdown coming on?"*

People expected him to reply: *"Consult a psychiatrist."* To their astonishment, he replied, *"Lock up your house, go across the railway tracks, find someone in need and do something to help that person."*

Good people, whoever you are, wherever you've come from and whatever your nationality or race may be, please band together with me to **make sure that nobody in our community suffers from hunger.**

With my kindest and best wishes to you,

Fr. Dan Madigan

Dear Friends:

Almost yearly I visit Ireland. While there **I stay in the house I was born in.** Our old home is still pretty much the same. However, everything else has changed.

Now the house has TV, telephone and washer/dryer. The farmyard has tractor, milking machine and silage pits. My nephews and nieces wear designer jeans, eat junk food and play with computers.

Ingenuity has brought my rural childhood surroundings a lot of change. And I am not at all convinced it's all for the better.

Back here in the US we are the epitome of progress. Human enterprise has given us unprecedented buildings and freeways.

But what about family life? What has it done to it? Let's look at some facts:

- Children are the poorest members of US society – one out of five children grows up in poverty.
- 40,000 children born each year in our country do not live to see their first birthday.
- Our infant mortality rate puts us last among 20 Western nations.
- An estimated 5.5 million US children under 12 are hungry, another 6 million are underfed.
- The rate of teenage suicide has tripled in 30 years.
- More than two and a half million children suffer physical, emotional or sexual abuse each year.
- More teenage boys die of gunshot wounds than from all natural causes combined.
- More than 25 percent of our teenagers drop out of school.

Friends, what am I asking of you? What can you do about this terrible situation? I feel that as long as you continue to see things with your heart, you will continue making a difference.

May God bless you for that inner kindness of yours.

With every good wish,

Fr. Dan Madigan

Dear Friends:

My Mom loved Mr. and Mrs. O'Connell. They taught her in the little two-room rural schoolhouse she attended. They were truly her mentors.

A classmate of my Mom's once handed Mrs. O'Connell a rather valuable coin. This youngster claimed she found it under a rock.

In the presence of the class Mrs. O'Connell cross-examined this child. **The little girl said she removed a rock from the footpath** that led from the school to its outdoor latrine. Mrs. O'Connell asked why she removed this rock. The child said she did so because she considered it a hazard.

Mrs. O'Connell complimented the little girl on her goodness then explained to all the class that it was indeed she herself who had put the coin there. She also explained that her purpose in doing so was to see who would remove the rock. Then she handed the coin back to the little Good Samaritan and said: *"Spend this on yourself."*

On a visit to Ireland some years ago I was told of the tragic death of one of my boyhood friends. This man was returning from town on a very cold day. He was driving his farm tractor. He was all bundled up. He didn't see the large stone in the middle of the narrow road when his front tire hit it his tractor overturned. He was killed instantly.

At his funeral a few of our neighbors felt very bad because they had passed by that stone. They had not done what my Mom's little friend had. They did not remove the hazard.

Friends, life has lots of hazards and pitfalls for all of us. We should try to remove them for each other. It's just the right thing to do.

May 1993 be a Happy New Year for you. May God reward you with great peace of mind. And may He assist you in the daily developing and enlarging of that kind heart of yours.

With every good wish,

Fr. Dan Madigan

Dear Friends:

Phillip Keller, a sheep rancher, has written a wonderful book called "A Shepherd Looks at Psalm 23."
In it he describes the sheep on the farm next to his, the sheep of a very negligent farmer.

> *"The tenant shepherd on the farm next to my first ranch was the most*
> *indifferent manager I had ever met. He wasn't concerned about the*
> *condition of his sheep. His land was neglected. He gave little or no*
> *time to his flock, letting them pretty well forage for themselves as best*
> *they could, both summer and winter. They fell prey to dogs, cougars and*
> *rustlers. Every year the poor creatures were forced to gnaw away at bare*
> *brown fields and impoverished pastures. Every winter there was a shortage*
> *of nourishing hay and wholesome grain to feed the hungry ewes.*
> *They only had muddy polluted water to drink. In my mind's eye*
> *I can still see them standing at the fence, huddled sadly in little knots*
> *staring wistfully through the wires at the rich pastures on the other side."*

Many times as I watch the lines of hungry people at our emergency food lockers, I think of Phillip Keller's neighboring sheep. Standing together, these poor, hungry, aching people look like a scroungy bunch of neglected sheep. Their need is so evident. Their hurt is so great. Their existence is a brutal contradiction to our wealthy country and our Christian beliefs.

Since childhood I have loved the picture of Our Lord with the lost sheep in His arms. This picture tells it all, the compassionate Christ and His expectations of us to be likewise.

Katherine Tynan's poem *"Sheep and Lambs"* also helps us to be kinder and more compassionate people.

All in the April evening,	Up in the blue, blue mountains
April airs were abroad,	Dewy pastures are sweet,
The sheep with their little lambs	Rest for the little bodies,
Passed me by on the road.	Rest for the little feet.
The lambs were weary, and crying	All in the April evening,
With a weak, human cry,	April airs were abroad,
I thought on the Lamb of God	I saw the sheep with their lambs.
Going meekly to die.	And thought on the Lamb of God.

May the good Lord bless and take care of you and yours.

With every good wish,

Fr. Dan Madigan

Dear Friends:

Saint Basil was born in Cappadocia in 330 and died in 379. Serving as Bishop of Caesarea, he was no diplomat as he explained the gospel the way he understood it. He said:

> *"The bread in your box belongs to the hungry;*
> *The cloak in your closet belongs to the naked;*
> ***The shoes you do not wear belong to the barefoot;***
> *The money in your vault belongs to the destitute."*

An old friend once asked Henry Ford, *"Why don't you ever buy any nuts and bolts from me?"* Mr. Ford replied, *"Heck, Joe, you never asked me."*

I myself fall somewhere between Saint Basil and Henry Ford's friend. I am not as strong as one or as shy as the other. I do ask. I ask often. And, yes, I do receive.

August is always a demanding month by way of requests for help. Our statistics bear this out. The reason for the increase is the added expense on parents of procuring clothing for children returning to school.

You, my friends, are givers. The Food Bank is the recipient of your charity. I promise you I will try to get the best possible mileage and accomplish the greatest amount of good that I can with your contributions.

May God bless you for your inner kindness.

With every good wish,

Fr. Dan.

Fr. Dan Madigan

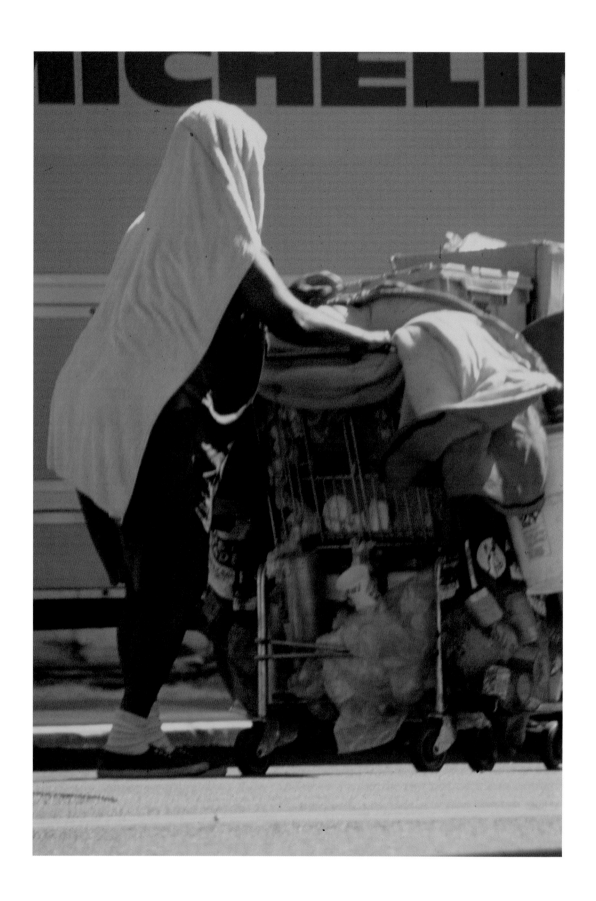

Dear Friends:

Common sense is a wonderful gift to have. Common sense tells us that two and two makes four. Common sense says if we have $10 and spend $5 we have only $5 left. Not $6. Not $7. Just $5.

Harry Truman said: *"If you can't stand the heat get out of the kitchen."* I feel that's what we are doing with common sense. We don't like what common sense is telling us; therefore, we don't use it anymore.

"Nemo Dat Quod Non Habet' is a common sense statement that comes to me from my seminary days. It says*: "You cannot give what you have not got."*

Nevertheless, this is what our country is doing. We are four trillion dollars in the hole and we are ignoring reality by clearly getting deeper and deeper in debt.

A trillion dollars meant nothing to me until discovering some years ago the following mathematical calculation. I have read this statement many times since. You will find it very sobering.

> *"Let's talk a trillion. For one trillion dollars, you could build a $75,000 house, place it on $5,000 worth of land, furnish it with $10,000 worth of furniture, put a $10,000 car in the garage and give all this to each and every family in Kansas, Missouri, Nebraska, Oklahoma, Colorado and Iowa.*
>
> *Having done this, you would still have enough left to build a $10 million hospital and a $10 million library in each of the 230 cities and towns throughout the six-state region.*
>
> *After having done all that, you would still have enough money left to build 500 schools at $10 million each for the communities in the region, and after having done all that you would still have enough left from the original trillion to put aside, at 10% annual interest, a sum of money that would pay a salary of $25,000 per year for an army of 10,000 nurses, the same salary for an army of 10,000 teachers, and an annual cash allowance of $5,000 for each and every family through the six-state region – not just for one year, but forever."*

So, my friends, the big question is **when will we ever learn?**

God bless and take care of yourselves.

With every good wish,

Fr. Dan Madigan

Dear Friends:

A recent study indicated that Sacramento children are becoming:
- Poorer
- Less educated
- Sicker
- And fewer efforts being made by official bureaucracy to save them

Oak Park Community has the:
- Highest infant mortality rate in Sacramento County
- Highest incidence of teenagers giving birth
- Worst rate for the immunization of children
- Highest numbers of low birth weights and drug and alcohol abuse in Sacramento County

I am sure you will agree that a family of four cannot live on a yearly income of $12,700. Yet one in every five children in our country are surviving – if not living – in such a household.

Daily we work with such families. They are where our food outlets are, in Oak Park and Del Paso Heights.

These families we see are truly hungry. They are hurting. Their children are in need of immediate help.

That's why we have designed a new program. **Our Mother/Baby Program will make a difference.** It will help salvage many of Sacramento's impoverished infants.

Don't let the magnitude of what we are up against keep you from stepping forward to help. Join us, please. The children we see need you.

As always, my kindest regards and best wishes to you,

Fr. Dan Madigan

Dear Friends:

American Indians tell the legend of a brave who found an eagle's egg one day. Not knowing what to do with it, he put it in a prairie chicken's nest. The prairie chicken sat on the egg and hatched it.

When the newly hatched eagle looked around, all he saw were prairie chickens, scratching and pecking for food. When they flew, he saw they rose only a few feet above the ground. So the young eagle followed the pattern of his companions, keeping close to the earth and venturing nowhere.

One day, glancing into the sky, he saw a magnificent bird wheeling high above the earth. As he watched, the bird seemed to be aiming for the sun, it flew so high. And then the great wings brought it swiftly circling, as if in delightful play, directly over the prairie chickens' grassy field.

> *"What kind if bird is that?"* he asked his companions.

> *"Oh, that's an eagle,"* an older chicken said. *"Eagles are the proudest, strongest, most royal of all birds. But don't think about them. Be happy on the ground with the rest of us chickens, for you're never going to fly like that one."*

The other chickens clucked in approval.

And so the eagle lived and died close to the ground, scratching for food like the prairie chickens.

He never knew his wings were meant for soaring in the sun. He never knew he had been destined to live on the highest mountain peak.

He never knew he was an eagle.

No one ever told him.

Yes – wings are for soaring. And we here at Sacramento Food Bank Services show people that they have wings and that they can fly. Please do join us.

With every good wish,

Fr. Dan Madigan

Dear Friends:

This letter is primarily for people my own age and older.

"Golden age," "senior citizens," "rest homes" and even "retirement" were alien words to me as a youngster. Back then additional years brought additional respect and venerability. Death was the only force that removed one from the stage of life.

Now all is changed. Our sophisticated society removes one quickly from life's stage. Impersonalization has taken over. Individual interaction is pushed into the background. The handshake agreement days of my Dad's generation are gone. This mass-production, conveyor-belt living system of ours needs to be looked at. Trees need to be seen rather than the forest. People need to be seen rather than the crowd.

St. Francis' advice, *"Grant that I may not so much seek to be understood as to understand,"* needs to be put into action.

Yes, we need to slow down. We need to smell the roses. We need to build bridges. We need to see to it that differences of race, creed, sex or religion make no difference to us. Please study Will Allen Dromgoole's poem. It will be the motto for our new Bridge Builders Club.

The Bridge Builders
An old man traveling a lone highway,
Came at the evening cold and gray,
To a chasm vast and deep and wide,
Through which was flowing a sullen tide.
The old man crossed in the twilight dim,
The sullen stream held no fears for him;
"Old man," cried a fellow pilgrim near,
 "You're wasting your time in building here.
Your journey will end with the closing day,
You never again will pass this way.
You have crossed the chasm deep and wide,
Why build you this bridge at eventide?"

The builder lifted his old gray head:
 "Good friend, in the patch I have come," he said,
"There followeth after me today
A youth whose feet must pass this way.
This stream which has been as naught to me
To that fair-haired youth may pitfall be.
He, too, must cross in the twilight dim –
Good friend, I am building this bridge for him."

With every good wish,

Fr. Dan Madigan

Dear Friends:

Sacramento Food Bank Services is now eighteen years old. It provides food, clothing, housing, literacy training and mother/baby care to people.

SFBS owes its ongoing existence to generous folks like yourself. **We have hundreds of volunteers** and thousands of donors. And while you wonderful people come from all ages, races and religions; the majority of you are children of the Great Depression.

The establishing of senior citizen groups at the churches of Sacred Heart and Immaculate Conception has certainly paid off for me. I gave you folks an organizational machine. You give SFBS numerous volunteer hours, much revenue and lots of mentoring time.

Yes, seniors have been and continue to be the lifeblood of SFBS. That's why I am renovating appropriate space and making plans for the establishment of a senior group called "The Senior Bridge Builders."

This new club will not treat senior people like fragile china. It will not offer pacifying, catering or accommodating programs. It will not indulge in stitchery, ceramics, macrame or flower arranging. Instead, it will be a club where experienced people meet, enjoy good food, good speakers, good recreation, and, most important of all, worthwhile projects.

This club will fly under the banner of the statement made by Cicero almost 2,000 years ago:

> *"Age is truly respectable in the man who guards himself from becoming the property of others, indicates his just right and maintains his proper authority to the last moments of his life."*

May God bless you for being an SFBS supporter.

With every good wish,

Fr. Dan Madigan

Dear Friends:

While it's rather pompous to feel that one has his or her act pretty much together and while it's judgmental to think of some others as dysfunctional, daily life shows that this division exists.

Also, while it's sobering to realize one has received many of life's advantages, it's equally realistic to know that many others received few or none at all.

I was born in Ireland in 1938. As a child I saw lots of scarcity, but never poverty.

Poverty's ingredients – hopelessness, helplessness, lack of values and lack of self-esteem – were alien to us. Parents, school, church and community kept positive thinking like the thoughts of Arthur O'Shaughnessy constantly before us:

> *"We are the music-makers,*
> *We are the dreamers of dreams,*
> *We are the movers and shakers,*
> *Of all the world, it seems."*

Sacramento's poor need the same breaks I received. They need more than handouts. **They need interaction** with caring and sensitive people. They need good friends who are willing to walk with them as they journey from destitution to self-actualization.

Here at SFBS we have programs that serve as vehicles for this type of interaction. Come, put your shoulder to the wheel and get even more involved with us. Remember our hurting neighbors need you.

So, friends of good will, let's say yes to the call of the poor. Let's make compassionate action and hands-on involvement guiding principles in our Capitol City.

God bless and take care of yourselves and please, please help others.

With every good wish,

Fr. Dan Madigan

130

Dear Friends:

God's message to us is simple: get involved, help the other person. Many people practice this belief.

Society's message is also clear: leave things alone, enjoy your high position on the seesaw. Many people also live by this way of thinking.

The following poem asks which side we support:

> I watched them tearing a building down,
> A gang of men in a busy town,
> With a ho-heave-ho and a lusty yell
> They swung a beam and the side wall fell.
> I asked the foreman, "Are those men skilled
> As the men you need if you had to build?"
> He gave a laugh and said, "No, indeed!
> I can easily wreck in a day or two
> What builders have taken years to do."
> I thought to myself as I went my way,
> Am I a builder who works with care,
> Measuring life by the rule or square?
> Am I shaping my deeds to a well-made plan,
> Patiently doing the best I can?
> Or am I wrecker who walks the town
> Content with the labor of tearing down?

Geese are not wreckers. They are not even competitors. They are team players. I know. During migration season I watch them fly over our church here in the Delta.

These wonderful creatures have discovered that by flying together they save a lot of energy. Geese flying in formation have a 70 percent aerodynamic advantage over a single goose trying to "fly on its own."

I also discovered that honking is not complaining. Honking is an array of supporting, encouraging and appreciating sounds.

So, my friends, be a builder. Come fly with us. If your schedule does not allow for active participation, then be one of our honkers.

With every good wish,

Fr. Dan Madigan

Dear Friends:

I have always believed that nature provided all people with common sense. Now I have changed my mind. Now I feel that Ralph Waldo Emerson was right when he said, *"Common Sense is as rare as Genius."*

All of us adults had to be taught, reared and mentored. Parents, family, books, school and church instilled a lot of sense into us.

Now I feel we have an obligation to pass this great chain of knowledge on to others.

I feel that our social services here at SFBS of feeding, clothing, housing, teaching and providing mother/ baby care has very little flesh on its bones if we are missing this "mentoring" element.

When I look back at my own rural upbringing and compare it with our sophisticated way of living today, I realize how impersonalized we have become. A Social Security number, a punched hole on an IBM card, a voice at the far end of the telephone keep us remote and detached.

You may object and say we are living in great times. Our freeways are fabulous. Our school buildings are spotless. Our hospitals are medical wonders.

True, but why are so many of our people alienated from the main stream of society? Why are so many wilting away in poverty, illiteracy and lack of values?

Individual attention is gone. Mass production has taken over. We see the forest. We miss the trees. We need to truly slow down and firmly believe that there is nothing more important in this great country of ours than a human being.

So, from here on out, I feel my goal in life is to teach people good sense. I will use any working tool I can lay my hands on to teach good values. Please continue to hang in there with us.

Remember, through our agency, SFBS, we are truly bettering people's lives.

With every good wish,

Fr. Dan Madigan.

Dear Friends:

Almost 30 years ago I came to Sacramento. It was much smaller then. Today it has grown, grown tremendously, and so have its problems.

During these years I have been privileged to work on both sides of the railway tracks. I have lived in Del Paso Heights, Oak Park and Sacramento's Fabulous Forties.

The difference between night and day describes what I saw. The best and worst of life stand side by side. No interaction between these two groups. **Both oblivious to each other's existence.**

In the greener pastures stood:
> *Home ownership – hard work – green lawns*
> *Discipline – motivation – responsibility*
> *Self-awareness – self-pride – self-expression*
> *Neighborhood accountability – career aspirations – college attendance*

Over the fence, so to speak, grew:
> *Idleness – homelessness – illiteracy*
> *Zero skills – zero work habits – zero aspirations*
> *Menial jobs – troubled homes – frazzled people*
> *Welfare dependence – dysfunctional adults – juvenile delinquents*

However, problems are only problems. They can always be solved with loving dedication. Please say "yes" to our appeal for volunteers. We really need you.

With every good wish,

Fr. Dan Madigan

Dear Friends:

Thanksgiving Day is almost upon us, and I, for one, have so much to be thankful for.

I love Ireland. I was born, reared and educated there. My parents rest there. My family lives there. I return there often and intend doing so as long as I am able.

But I also have a soft spot for Sacramento. In fact, I love it dearly. It's been my home for close to 30 years. It's where I do my work. And where I intend ending my days.

I am truly blessed with job fulfillment. Each morning as I drive to work I know the day will bring:

- 800 families for food
- 100 families for clothing
- 60 moms will bring their babies for special care
- 45 students and their teachers will come to our literacy center
- 12 families will be housed and mentored
- **10,000 pounds of food will enter our warehouse**
- 130 volunteers will come to work

Yes, indeed, through the development of:

- 800 volunteers
- 4,500 donors
- warehouses, dwelling houses, trucks, forklifts, refrigerators/freezers
- tremendous buying power
- and prayerful persuasion

We will accomplish what experts tell us is a $10 million a year operation.

And while it's a mind boggling fact that we do all this work with a million dollar cash flow, the most wonderful part of the story is that at least 90 percent of all our money comes from you, the recipients of this newsletter.

So, Sacramentans, I truly thank God on this Thanksgiving Day for the great privilege I have of walking among you.

God bless and take care of you.

With every good wish,

Fr. Dan Madigan

Dear Friends:

Recently I visited my old homestead in Ireland. In a way nothing has changed. Robins, sparrows, thrushes, wrens, blackbirds, jackdaws, and blue tits sing, twitter and hop around the farmyard. Crows, magpies, pigeons, snipe and curlews were in the fields. According to my brothers, lots of rabbits, hares, foxes and badgers are still around.

But what about the overseas visitors? Do they still come to Ireland? The swallows, they informed me, are as plentiful as ever, yet the corncrake is almost completely extinct. The cuckoo is quickly decreasing.

I was sad to hear about the corncrake. I have lots of childhood memories of falling asleep to their raucous cries "AIC-AIC" coming from the cover of the nearby meadows. Cuckoos came to Ireland from Africa. Hearing of their decline did not bother me. I never liked those birds. I considered their lifestyle unacceptable.

As children we were raised to pull our own load in life, to play fair in all dealings with people, to be totally responsible for our actions, and to respect others' property as a holy sanctuary never to be touch.

The cuckoo broke all these rules. She refused to hatch her own eggs. She cunningly placed them in the nests of other birds. Later, demanding total attention for itself, her offspring threw all the other rightful occupants from the nest, and when ready to fly departed uncaringly from its frustrated parents.

To me a cuckoo lifestyle is shameful. It is unacceptable for birds, unacceptable for animals, and, certainly, unacceptable for human beings.

May the good Lord take care of you as you take care of others.

With every good wish,

Fr. Dan Madigan

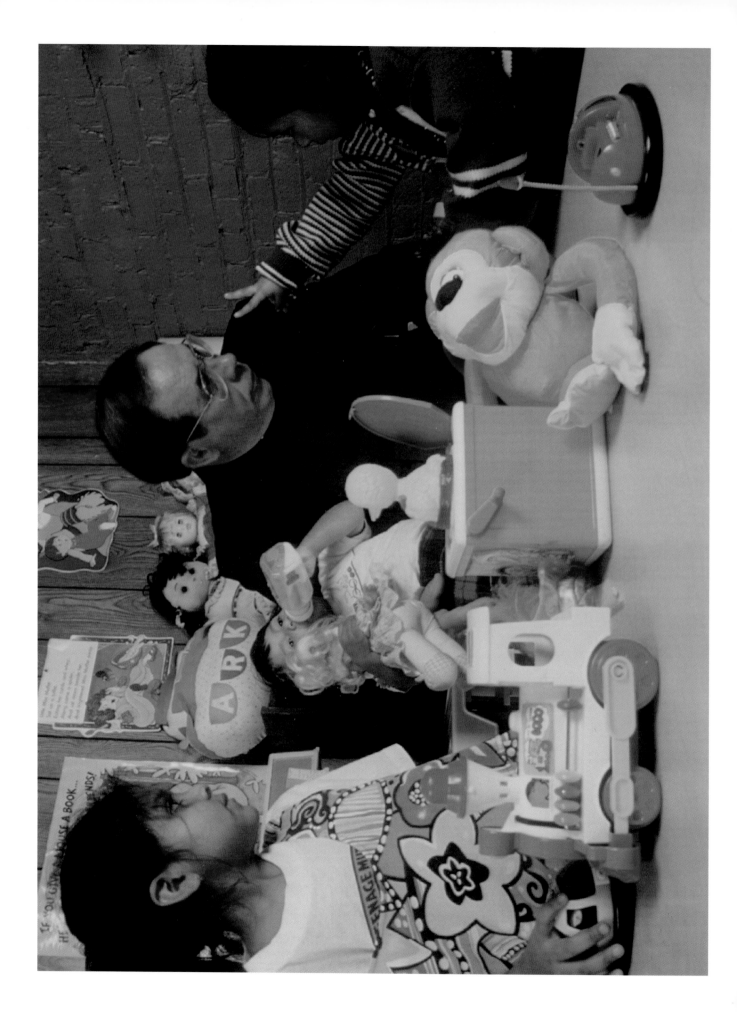

Dear Friends:

I have fond memories of 1993. Eight hundred of you gave us countless hours of volunteer work. Four thousand of you contributed a million dollars in cash. Our agency delivered ten million dollars in social services.

Yes, it's a real privilege to captain a ship where dollar bills are turned into tens. Where we not only believe in miracles, but watch them happen before our eyes.

Our multiplication formula worked well on the day prior to Thanksgiving. We fed 2000 families. We gave each a $50 box of food. We did it all for $5,300.

Multiplication worked even better at Christmas. **Two thousand kids received gifts from us and all at zero cost to our operation.**

Yes, the miracle is still going on. Generous Sacramento businesses, offices, schools, churches, clubs and organizations are presently filling barrels with food for our Holiday Spirit of Giving Drive. We expect to net 300,000 pounds of food which, if purchased at market value, would cost around $300,000.

Today I officiated at a funeral. I read Psalm 23. I listened to the prophet say, *"Though I walk in the valley of darkness I fear no evil for You are with me."*

As I drove back to the Food Bank I found myself thinking how true that prayer is. Why should I, who has the Lord rooting for our Food Bank, worry about 1994?

May God bless you all. You are truly, truly wonderful people.

With every good wish,

Fr. Dan Madigan

Dear Friends:

There seems to be a strong public opinion today that California is taking a nosedive. That crime, gangs, narcotics, poverty and homelessness are on the increase while strong family life is quickly deteriorating.

The United Nations is proclaiming this year of 1994 as *"The Year of the Family."* It seems all countries crave the return of the strong parenting days of old.

We here at SFBS feed, clothe, house and educate people. We run baby programs and senior programs. But by far the most important thing we do is build bridges, linkages, alliances and mentoring between people who have and people who have not.

Yes, as far as I can see, mentoring is the only true answer. Osmosis works and works well. "Haves" and "Have Nots" have everything to do with the possession of, or lack of, good rearing, healthy discipline and proper values. "Haves" and "Have Nots" have much less to do with mere material possessions.

So, if you agree with my thinking please join us. **We will give you the opportunity for the daily dispensing of services.** Above all, we will give you the opportunity of imparting to people our philosophy of self-empowerment.

With every good wish,

Fr. Dan Madigan

Dear Friends:

On this upcoming **St. Patrick's Day** we will hear a lot about Irish joviality – leprechauns, Blarney Stone, Guinness Stout and Bailey's Irish Cream. We may even hear about some Irish products such as Waterford crystal, Aran sweaters, Donegal tweed and Claddagh jewelry but what about the real Ireland? How much does the average American know about it?

Ireland is an island. Territorially, it's one-fifth the size of the State of California. Climatically, it's decently temperate despite its northern position on the globe. Its mildness of weather is due to the kindness of the Atlantic Gulf Stream. Politically, its self-governed 26 counties live in tranquillity while its foreign-occupied six northern counties live in chaos.

In 432 St. Patrick brought Christianity to Ireland. The Irish took to this new way of life like ducks to water. So much so that for many centuries Ireland became known throughout Europe as *"The Island of Saints and Scholars."* The Book of Kells, the Ardagh Chalice and the Cross of Cong were all products of this age.

Everything changed in the sixteenth century when England stripped Ireland of its religious freedom. In the seventeenth century she took away its economic freedom. By the eighteenth century the vast majority of Irish were reduced to living as tenant peasants working for absentee landlords and accountable to on-site hatchet men. It was then that the Great Famine struck.

The ghastliness of the Potato Famine – Ireland's Via Dolorosa – will forever be indelibly imprinted in the minds of her people. Irish beef, grain and dairy products belonged to the landlord, the despised potato to the tenant, and it was the potato crop that rotted.

Eviction, starvation, workhouses and mass graves were the lot of most who stayed in Ireland. Coffin ships, dreadful diseases and sea burials were the fate of many of its deportees. For those who made it to American and Canadian soil, there awaited delousing centers, tenement slums, deep scorn and window notices that read, *"No Irish Need Apply."*

But apply they did. And they got the jobs no one else would do. Their sons and daughters did better and climbed the social and economic ladder higher and higher. So today in real estate and banking, in politics and industry, and in every profession imaginable, the Irish-Americans have gone right to the top.

Yes, today forty-two million Americans claim Irish ancestry and outnumber the Irish in Ireland by more than ten to one. Yes, today thirty-five percent of corporate America is controlled by Irish-Americans.

Fellow Irish-Americans, let's remember the famine's appalling suffering, not with bitterness and hatred but with the resolve that *"we will never do unto others the wrong that was done to our own."*

Fellow American people, let's all make it a part of our life to daily advocate for all people the policies of justice and compassion.

With every good wish,

Fr. Dan Madigan

146

Dear Friends:

I was raised in a family with two parents, four brothers and four sisters. Our family was not run by a committee. Neither were our family rules drawn up by consensus. **Mom and Dad** were clearly in charge. Mom was the vocal leader. Dad was the quieter partner.

Now while both my parents were gentle, kind and loving, they were, nevertheless, far removed from being wishy-washy. We kids always knew where we stood with them. Conduct standards were well defined. Accountability was demanded. Daily workloads were expected to be accomplished. Laziness was unacceptable. Aspirations were always encouraged.

Harry Truman said, *"Leadership is getting people to do things they don't want to do."* If this is so, then my Mom was a Napoleon.

General Mark Clark said *"Leadership is walking the extra mile."* If this is true, my Dad was a Mother Teresa of Calcutta.

Grandparents and great grandparents, you are a remarkable people. You lived through history's Great Depression. You have a tremendous amount of knowledge in your heads; much love in your hearts, and great values in your system. All younger generations need to hear from you.

Grandparents, great grandparents, you are not fragile china. You are not over the hill. You are totally alive. You have lots and lots to offer. I need your help in the putting together of our new Oak Park Family Center. Please give me a call.

With every good wish,

Fr. Dan Madigan

JULY 1994

Dear Friends:

As a youngster in rural Ireland I saw fetters and hobbles used. These chains were placed on the feet of horses or bulls to impede their movement. Their use always bothered me.

Today TV shows us shackles and manacles. **Human beings in restraints. Reminders that in a way we all have failed.**

The words *"yoke"* and *"galling chain"* always make me cringe. Subjection, bondage and servitude should simply never exist.

But exist they do. And every day we see around us fetters, hobbles, shackles, manacles, yokes and galling chains. We see them enslave people of all races, ages and creeds. We quickly learn that the majority of these restraints are inherited by birth. Others are self-imposed.

Gall is a sore on the skin caused by rubbing, friction or chafing. Illiteracy, poverty, addiction and low self-esteem are galls. Galls are very difficult to cure. Loving, dedicated mentors are needed to do the job.

The good Lord said, *"My yoke is easy and my burden is light."* At least that's the way He wants it to be. And that's why He asks us to be good to each other.

So, friends, please do continue to help as you have over the years. Together we are making a difference in the lives of many hurting families.

Also, take good care of yourselves and let that inner goodness of yours grow and grow.

With every good wish,

Fr. Dan Madigan

Dear Friends:

Volunteers are the lifeblood of Sacramento Food Bank Services. SFBS truly does what it does because of the hundreds of people that give it time, talent and money.

While giving a lecture on mental health Dr. Karl Menninger, the famous psychiatrist, was once asked the question, *"What would you advise a person to do if that person felt a nervous breakdown coming on?"* Most people expected Menninger to say, *"Consult a psychiatrist."* To their astonishment he replied, *"Lock up your house, go across the railroad tracks, find someone in need and help him."*

Yes, indeed, studies have shown that people who volunteer and participate in community activities live longer and healthier lives than those who isolate themselves with their problems.

When making presentations to groups, I am often asked, *"Why not involve the people who come to us for assistance in our actual work?"* My answer is, *"If the distribution of services was the only goal of SFBS then most people would qualify to become a volunteer; however, this is not the case."*

SFBS has a planned strategy underscoring all of its services. It is that of involving volunteers of high integrity in **"mentoring," "bridge-building,"** and **"walking hand-in-hand"** with hurting people.

Because of our philosophy we demand that our volunteers be people of uncompromising honesty. They also have to possess great sensitivity, compassion, empathy and people skills.

We fully realize that not all people are ready for this noble work. However, we do hope that with a little help from us they will one day be able and willing to accept this challenge.

In the meantime, it's a question of those of us who have had some real breaks in life helping those our sisters and brothers who were less fortunate than we. Please contact us if you have some volunteer time to give us.

Take care of yourself and may God truly bless you.

With every good wish,

Fr. Dan Madigan

Dear Friends:

Every day Sacramento Food Bank Services sees hundreds and hundreds of impoverished people. They come to us because they are experiencing severe shortage. In other words, they have "no fish" to eat.

We give them fish. Not as much as they need, but as much as we can afford.

Several years ago we began to ask ourselves, *"Why don't these folks know how to fish?"* As a result of our questioning we started programs in mentoring, counseling and teaching.

Today we do teach people the art of fishing. Yes, today we feel we are making a huge difference in the lives of many folks.

However, what worries me most is the large number of people who come to us who are able to fish. People who can genuinely say what the Apostles said many years ago, *"Lord, we have been hard at it all night long and have caught nothing."*

Minimum wage just doesn't cut it any more. You can't raise a family on a McDonald's or Burger King or Taco Bell salary. Yet many people are doing just that.

SFBS has always helped the underdog. But times have changed and dysfunctional people are now in the minority. The majority we encounter are struggling with utility bills, rent payments, family rearing and inadequate income.

So, daily we see lots and lots of the hurt of the working poor. Thank God, daily we also see lots and lots of community understanding, compassion and support.

July, August and September were lean months for us financially. July, August and September put us in the red. However, I am praying that the giving months of November and December will help us back on our feet. Please help us to whatever extent you can.

May God take care of you and yours in this Thanksgiving season.

With every good wish,

Fr. Dan Madigan

154

Dear Friends:

Nineteen years ago I helped put together a community food locker.

Today this operation has grown from food to multiple services, from handouts to handups, from giving people fish to teaching them how to fish.

Today this grassroots organization has a volunteer corps of 800 and a staff of 16. The Food Bank has a one and a quarter million dollar operating budget, 93% of which comes from the pockets of Sacramentans.

In this past year of 1994 Sacramento Food Bank Services:

SERVED	- 650,200 people with take home food
FED	- Sunday lunch to 38,902 adults and 41,535 children
CLOTHED	- 47,341 people with 200,506 articles of clothing
HOUSED	- 21 families in the Food Bank's 12 homes
EDUCATED	- 125 students in reading and writing English and in learning job skills
SUPPLIED	- 18,988 babies with food, formula and diapers
MENTORED	- 15,124 moms through parental education classes
GLEANED	- 9,600 volunteer hours from the members of its Bridge Builders club
ESTABLISHED	- A Family Learning Center and a Recycling program

In addition to donations of hard cash and volunteers, SFBS is also the recipient of millions of pounds of food, tons of clothing, houses, automobiles and furniture. Volunteers donate their time and skills for major building repair jobs.

Several managerial people have assured SFBS that it is yearly producing ten million dollars worth of services to the Sacramento community.

To you, dear reader, who helps us so much, I send my fondest regards and deep appreciation.

Take care and may God bless you.

With every good wish,

Fr. Dan Madigan

Dear Friends:

Celebrities are celebrities because of high visibility and much publicity. Heroes are heroes because of noble character, uncompromising honesty, strong courage and ethical behavior.

All heroes deserve to be celebrities. But not all celebrities qualify for the badge of heroism.

It is very important that our children know the difference between heroes and celebrities. Make sure you explain it to them.

My parents were heroes. They gave my sisters, brothers and me a comfortable nest, security, fond memories, friendship, hospitality and family togetherness. Edgar Guest's poem, "Only a Dad", describes my Dad very well.

> *Only a dad with a tired face, coming home from the daily race,*
> *Bringing little of gold or fame, to show how well he has played the game;*
> *But glad in his heart that his own rejoice, to see him come and to hear his voice.*
>
> *Only a dad with a brood of four, one of ten million men or more,*
> *Plodding along in the daily strife, bearing the whips and the scorns of life,*
> *With never a whimper of pain or hate, for the sake of those who at home await.*
>
> *Only a dad, neither rich nor proud, merely one of the surging crowd,*
> *Toiling, striving from day to day, facing whatever may come his way.*
> *Silent whenever the harsh condemn, and bearing it all for the love of them.*
>
> *Only a dad but he gives his all, to smooth the way for his children small,*
> *Doing with courage stern and grim, the deeds that his father did for him.*
> This is the line that for him I pen. **Only a dad, but the best of men."**

You, my friends, are also the very best of people. You are part of what we do here at Sacramento Food Bank Services. And I thank you from the bottom of my heart for your generosity.

May God truly bless you.

With every good wish,

Fr. Dan Madigan

Dear Friends:

During the building of the Golden Gate Bridge in San Francisco there were no safety devices to prevent the workers from falling to their death. As a consequence twenty three men fell and died. Eventually a huge safety net was erected. The result was wonderful. Not alone did it save lives, but it increased work productivity by twenty-five percent.

Poor families have no safety net. They live in constant fear. Lack of an adequate income disintegrates them, wearing away their morale and self-esteem.

These shattered families need more than a homeless shelter or a food locker or a soup kitchen. They need friends. MENTORS. Common sense people who can lead them from where they are to where they should be. Dedicated folks who will walk with them, step by step, as they journey from destitution to self-actualization.

When hungry and destitute people come to our door we greet them with "hand out" hospitality.

Before they leave we gently tell them of our "hand up" programs. Some return. And through involvement with us many do get back on their feet.

The recipe for escaping poverty is simple. Finish high school. Get a job. Stay in the labor market. Get married as an adult. Stay married.

The media constantly outlines our country's ills such as crime, drugs, poverty, illiteracy, and homelessness. Seldom does it mention what may well be one of our biggest and most basic problems, illegitimacy.

A recent study found that children born to females who finished high school, who married and reached age twenty before having their first child, lived in poor households at a rate of 8%. By contrast children born to mothers who did not finish high school, who did not marry, and who gave birth in their teens, had a poverty rate of 79%.

Catch-22 has become a common phrase. It means being boxed in, having no escape options, no solutions.

We here at SFBS work with Catch-22 people. Through your help and generosity we many times remove horrendous obstacles, entrapments and dilemmas for them.

Please pray about becoming a mentor. We need you. The poor need you. Yes, together we will make a big difference for many Sacramento families.

With every good wish,

Fr. Dan Madigan

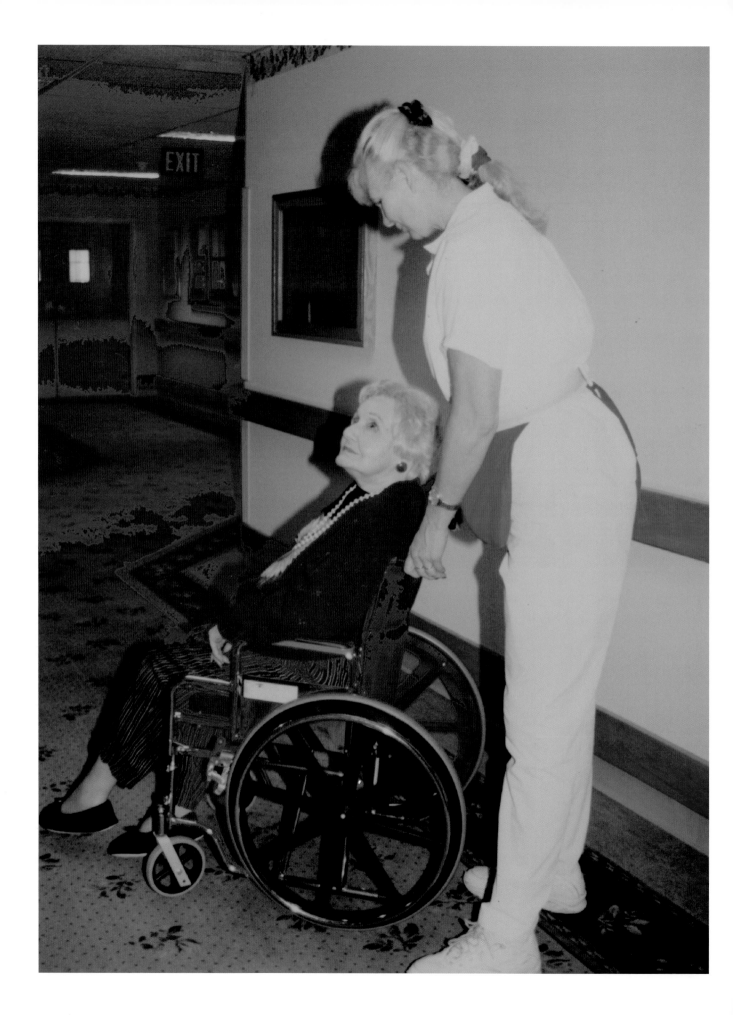

Dear Friends:

In January 1979 I visited my sister and her husband and family in western Australia. It was a difficult visit as my sister, Bridie, who was only 53 years of age was dying of cancer.

While there I ran across the following poem which I have kept ever since and have, over the years, read it many times. It carries a very strong message. I hope that you find it as thought-provoking as I do.

__What do you see, nurse,__ what do you see?
What are you thinking when looking at me –
A crabbit old woman, not very wise,
Uncertain of habit, with faraway eyes.

Who dribbles her food and makes no reply
When you say in a loud voice, "I do wish you'd try."
Who seems not to notice the things that you do,
And forever is losing a stocking or shoe.

Who unresisting or not, lets you do as you will,
With bathing, and feeding, the long day to fill.
Is that what you're thinking, is that what you see?
Then open your eyes, nurse, you're not looking at me!

I'll tell you who I am, as I sit here SO still,
As I muse at your bidding, as I eat at your will.
I am a small child of ten, with a father and mother,
Brothers and sisters, who love one another.

A young girl of eighteen, with wings on her feet,
Dreaming that soon now a lover she'll meet,
A bride now at twenty – my heart gives a leap,
Remembering the vows that I promised to keep.

At twenty-five now, I have young of my own,
Who need me to build them a secure, happy home,
A woman of thirty, my young now grow fast,
Bound to each other with ties that should last.

At forty, my young sons have grown and are gone,
But my man's still beside me to see I don't mourn.
At fifty, once more babies around my knee,
Again, we know children, my loved one and me.

Dark days are upon me, my husband is dead,
I look at the future, I shudder with dread.
For all my young are rearing young of their own,
And I think of the years and the love that I've known.

I'm an old woman now and nature is cruel –
'Tis her jest to make old age look like a fool.
The body it crumbles, grace and vigor depart,
There is now a stone where I once had a heart.

But inside this old carcass a young girl still dwells,
And now and again, my battered heart swells..
I remember the joys, I remember the pain,
And I'm in love and living life over again.

I think of the years all too few – gone too fast,
And accept the stark fact that nothing can last.
So open your eyes, nurse, open and see
Not a crabbit old woman, look closer – see ME.

Upon retirement all seniors should assume the same outlook as that of Maggie Kuhn, the lady who founded the Grey Panthers. Here's what she had to say: *"We have a lot to offer society, we old folks. We're not finished, or washed up, or out to pasture. We have ideas, many ideas, and if anybody asks us, we're willing to share out ideas."*

When you retire, make it clear to everyone that you have ongoing tasks to perform, missions to accomplish, dreams to be realized, and a powerhouse of knowledge, integrity and encouragement to pass on to anyone who is willing to listen.

God bless you older people. You are giants in my eyes.

With every good wish,

Fr. Dan Madigan

Dear Friends:

My seminary training gave me answers to all questions. While thirty years in the priesthood has removed that secure platform, these same thirty years have introduced me to a much kinder God than the one I knew as a youngster.

Fr. Joseph Girzone, the author of Joshua, has this to say about religion:

> *For sixteen centuries we have associated religion with church buildings and institutional structures. When we think of the Church, we instinctively think of bricks and steel, of dignitaries in flowing robes and ornate ritual. Since childhood these images have been engraved in our memories. They are changeless, immutable, everlasting. To think of altering them shakes people's faith.*
>
> *Yet, in all the Gospel stories Jesus' way of life and the flow of His teachings had nothing to do with buildings or structures or complex rituals. He did attend the synagogue faithfully. He did attend the temple services for the sacred feasts. But He once remarked that true worship is not in buildings but in the sincerity of our lives and the devotion of our hearts.*
>
> *His followers for over two hundred years followed that simple way of worshipping God by gathering in unadorned family liturgies and caring for each other's needs. But then came the Roman Emperors who decided to do God a favor and gather Christ's followers into what became the imperial religion of Rome. From then on Christianity became a thing of grandeur and pageantry. The simple Jesus was lost, His message became enshrined in finely chiseled theological concepts.*
>
> *On rare occasions through the centuries, the Spirit of God managed to break through the hard crust of religion and inspire individuals, usually simple, docile souls, to discover for themselves the real Jesus and to act out in their own lives the life-style set forth by the Master. St. Francis was one. Damian the Leper another, as well as **Mother Teresa** and Gandhi.*

Friends, if you feel in any way alienated from God please meditate on the following old Spiritual. It brings me much consolation. I hope it will do the same for you.

> *He didn't bring us this far to leave us;*
> *He didn't teach us to swim to let us drown;*
> *He didn't build His home in us to move away;*
> *He didn't lift us up to let us down.*

So take care of yourselves. Stop worrying. And remember God is truly your pal.

With every good wish,

Fr. Dan Madigan

Dear Friends:

Every language possesses a large store of proverbs. The following ones pertain to the characteristics of parents and their offspring.

Apples don't fall far from the tree
It is natural for the fawn of a deer to have fleetness
What would you expect from a cat but a kitten
Birds of the same feather fly together
And whether it be black, dun or brown, it is its own kid the goat loves

Now how about you? What was your upbringing like? Were you born a gosling, a chicken or a turkey? Irish writer, Alice Taylor, explains the difference:

The goose liked to make her own nest and line it inside with soft down.
The gander for his part was a most responsible father and guarded his goose
on the nest; if you came too close he flapped his wings and stretched out his
long neck to bite you. The young goslings were fluffy and yellow as butter
and the goose and gander led them daily to the water where they all washed
and swam around happily. But the males in the turkey and hen families were
irresponsible fathers; once they had made their original contribution they
disclaimed all responsibility for the consequences.

Great care had to be taken of the baby turkeys as they were a bit stupid and
unlike the chickens and goslings had a tendency to get lost. The goose was
a very good mother and she had a strong family unit working for her; the
ordinary hen was the head of a one-parent family but her mothering instinct
was fantastic. The turkey on the other hand had neither factor going for
her; she was on her own and she was not unduly concerned about the
well-being of her young. She needed a strong social welfare system to
back her up and, of course, we provided that. ***Minding the turkeys was***
one of the chores of my young days. *They had endless ways of going wrong.*
If they fell on their backs they could not right themselves; they could ramble
off through the long grass and, with no sense of direction, get totally lost, and
their mother would never bother to answer their plaintive 'peep peep'.

So, good reader, if you had a great upbringing, truly thank God for it. In gratitude embrace the helping and uplifting of less fortunate people. And please consider getting involved with SFBS as a volunteer.

With every good wish,

Fr. Dan Madigan

Dear Friends:

Sacramento Food Bank Services is located on 34th Street and 3rd Avenue in Oak Park. Older Sacramentans remember our neighborhood as much different than it is today. In the not-too-far distant past, handsome homes and well-kept streets surrounded McClatchy Park. Broadway boasted first-class dress shops and prosperous businesses. Our headquarters flourished under the well-known community figure, Charlie Arata.

It seemed unthinkable then that this upper middle-class suburb would ever deteriorate, but in the mid-1960s two intercepting freeways cut into the heart of this neighborhood. Scores of fine homes were eliminated and hundreds of families moved away. With them went better stores and firms, turning a gracious residential district into a very poor area.

When I talk with the less fortunate of our clients and note the absence of self-esteem and their inadequacies such as illiteracy, I marvel at the breaks I have had through no merit of my own. I think of the gift I had in a loving family and good home.

As I grew and matured, my roots branched out onto that other family, the school. There I had excellent teachers who challenged me to perform and deliver. Like the eaglet hatched by chickens in the old Indian legend, I might have been content to remain earthbound and wingless if caring parents had not persuaded me I could fly.

Is it time for you and for me to pay our dues? Freely gifted at birth, we have been continually blessed with friends and opportunities, thanks to God's providence. If He secretly hoped we would pass those blessings on, He took a gamble on us, for human nature likes to credit success to its own capabilities and efforts. He has the right to expect accountability from the mature people we have become, and now this Food Bank and its programs present another kind of opportunity – the chance to repay.

Friends, I am now asking you to reaffirm your commitment to the Sacramento Food Bank Family. Rabindranath Tagore, the East Indian philosopher/poet, said, *"Every child who is born comes with the message that God is not yet discouraged with mankind."* Help us to prove him right. Help us to give these children, who have so many strikes against them, the affirmation they need to value themselves. Help us to assure them they can fly.

SFBS is doing its utmost to be an oasis of permanence, peace and order here in the Oak Park district. Daily we strive not only to give families fish, but also to teach them how to fish. Thank God we are having great success. Please continue to hang in there with us.

With every good wish,

Fr. Dan Madigan

170

Dear Friends:

Here is a little something I gleaned from a friend. It is a beautiful piece of writing and has a great message. I want ever so much to give its author credit for this little masterpiece, but I cannot come up with that information.

> A water bearer in India had two large pots, each hung on each end of a pole which he carried across his neck. One of the pots had a crack in it, and while the other pot was perfect and always delivered a full portion of water at the end of the long walk from the stream to the master's house, the cracked pot arrived only half full. For a full two years this went on daily, with the bearer delivering only one and a half pots full of water in his master's house. Of course, the perfect pot was proud of its accomplishments, perfect to the end of which it was made.

> But **the poor cracked pot** was ashamed of its own imperfection, and miserable that it was able to accomplish only half of what it had been made to do. After two years of what it perceived to be a bitter failure, it spoke to the water bearer one day by the stream. 'I am ashamed of myself, and I want to apologize to you.' 'Why?' asked the bearer. 'What are you ashamed of?' 'I have been able, for these past two years, to deliver only half my load because this crack in my side causes water to leak out all the way back to your master's house. Because of my flaws you have to do all of this work, and you don't get full value from your efforts,' the pot said.

> The water bearer felt sorry for the old cracked pot, and in his compassion he said, 'As we return to the master's house, I want you to notice the beautiful flowers along the patch.' Indeed, as they went up the hill, the old cracked pot took notice of the sun warming the beautiful wild flowers on the side of the patch, and this cheered it some. But at the end of the trail, it still felt bad because it had leaked out half its load, and so again the pot apologized to the bearer for its failure.

> The bearer said to the pot, 'Did you notice that there were flowers only on your side of your patch, but not on the other pot's side? That's because I have always known about your flaw, and I took advantage of it. I planted flower seeds on your side of the patch, and everyday while we walked back from the stream you've watered them. For two years I have been able to pick these beautiful flowers to decorate my master's table. Without you being just the way you are, he would not have this beauty to grace his house.'

Each of us has his or her own flaws. We are all cracked pots, but despite our flaws God loves us all and we should learn to accept the little cracks in each other's lives.

With every good wish,

Fr. Dan Madigan

Dear Friends:

In Ireland "Twenty Years-A-Growing" is considered a classic. Recently I read its English translation and with nostalgia recalled my youthful study of it in its original Gaelic version "Fiche Blian Ag Fas."

"Twenty Years-A-Growing" is now an appropriate title for our Food Bank. In January we will celebrate its twenty year milestone.

Over these past twenty years we have grown much. Experience and prayerful thinking have widened our mission. We still feed, clothe, and house people. But now we **educate them and help move them along with their lives.**

Daily we build up self-worth, self-confidence, and self-esteem. Daily we show people that they can do better. Daily we prove to them that our dedication is unselfish and our interest in their welfare is totally reliable.

Yes, indeed, SFBS daily teaches people kindness, patience, tolerance, honesty, compassion and a work ethic.

Each day SFBS teaches a higher standard of values. And each day SFBS helps those people reach their full potential.

This is the Food Bank you support. I thank you from the bottom of my heart and ask that if it is possible for you to write us a check this Christmas season please do so. We truly need it. May God bless you.

With every good wish,

Fr. Dan Madigan

Dear Friends:

People seldom ask me where I hail from. My accent gives me away. Twenty-seven years of Sacramento living hasn't put a ding in my Irish brogue.

"An Gorta Mor" is a sad Gaelic expression. It means the Great Hunger, The Irish Potato Famine. An Gorta Mor means starvation, destitution, evictions and shallow graves. It means two million people dying in hovels, roads and ditches of Ireland. It means that in the middle of the potato rot, shiploads of wheat, oats and flour were leaving the Irish ports for foreign destinations. It means thousands of people boarding "coffin ships" for the United States in the desperate hope of finding a better life.

Since childhood I wanted to come to the United States. The noble words of the Constitution and the inspirational thoughts on the Statue of Liberty called out to me. I longed to live in the land that opened its arms in 1846 and 1847 to the wretched refuse of my famine-torn country. I wanted to live my life where all people are created equal, where all people enjoy the inalienable rights of life, liberty and the pursuit of happiness.

My first exposure to working in this community was in Del Paso Heights in the 1960s. On many late evenings people knocked on the rectory door because a loved one had been drafted and was being sent to Vietnam. They came for consolation. In the 1980s I again answered the late evening knock at the rectory door. This time it was in Oak Park, and there was still a war on – a new war, the war of nothing to eat, nowhere to sleep, the war of persistent poverty. One out of every four children in Sacramento County lives in a welfare family. They live in poverty, they are often hungry, they are sometimes homeless.

Starvation may be alien to our capital city but malnutrition is not. Daily we see diets that help fill baby's stomachs but do little to nourish their bodies. Daily we see what poverty and illiteracy are doing to families. It disintegrates them. It wears away their morale and self-esteem. It has disastrous effects on their physical and emotional well-being. It can lead to some awfully serious health ailments.

The Irish famine did not have to happen. There was a great deal of food in Ireland. There was lots of knowledge and many studies, commissions, reports and resolutions, but there was no action, no relief. Millions died.

I pray for the day when all the people of our country will stand up and say, "Poverty in the U.S.A. is unacceptable. Illiteracy is unacceptable. Homelessness is unacceptable."

I also pray for the day when churches will get down into the trenches and lift up people. We need to do more than just feed, house and clothe people. We need to take them by the hand and befriend, mentor and counsel them. We need to lead them from where they are to where they should be.

With every good wish,

Fr. Dan Madigan

Dear Friends:

Since childhood I have regarded Religion and Spirituality as synonymous. And while this thinking may very well be true, years of working at SFBS has exposed me to numerous people who are deeply spiritual but who are not associated with any given religious group.

True spirituality is indeed a dangerous concept. **It cost the Good Lord His life.**

English mystery writer, Dorothy L. Sayers, says: *"Christ was tender to the unfortunate, patient with honest inquirers, and humble before Heaven; but He insulted respectable clergymen by calling them hypocrites; He referred to King Herod as 'that fox'; He went to parties in disreputable company and was looked upon by religious bureaucrats as a 'gluttonous man and a winebibber, a friend of publicans and sinners.' He assaulted indignant tradesmen and threw them and their belongings out of the temple. He showed no proper deference for wealth and social position."*

Dorothy Sayers goes on to say: *"Officialdom felt that the established order of things would be more secure without Him. So they did away with God in the name of peace and quietness."*

Christ's message was certainly not about grandeur, pageantry or bureaucracy. It was about uplifting people. It was about trying to make people's lives easier and more nobler. And that's what we must do during this great penitential season of Lent. We must help families get back on their feet.

Friends, be assured that any donation made to SFBS in honor of Lent/Easter/St. Patrick's Day or for any other private intention will be put to very good use. With your donation we will truly accomplish much good.

With every good wish,

Fr. Dan Madigan

Dear Friends:

Bishop Fulton Sheen said: *"I would rather see a sermon that hear one."*

Will Rogers said: *"Know what you are doing. Love what you are doing. Believe in what you are doing."*

All social service agencies love and believe in what they do, but are all social service agencies fully aware of what they are truly trying to accomplish?

I say this because experience has shown me that many poor people are content to receive catering help. Many agencies feel perfectly fulfilled in the mere rendering of such a service.

However, the reality is what are both sides accomplishing? Pauperization is flourishing. Self-actualization is stagnant. Self-esteem and ethical values are not even issues.

I also question if the Government can indeed teach moral values. I question even further if agencies which feed heavily from Government troughs are rendered impotent by that very reliance.

This is the kind of thinking that has motivated me over these past twenty years to bypass bureaucracy and to turn to church pews, civic organizations and individual folks for **hands-on volunteer help.** I embrace the Sacramento populace for our needed financial support.

Sacramentans – you have always been there for us, and, of course, we do what we do because of you. May God bless and take care of you.

With every good wish,

Fr. Dan Madigan

Dear Friends:

When I came to this country in 1966 there was economic growth, job security, livable wages and many opportunities for advancement.

Today, with the exception of a very successful minority many other people seem to be just limping along.

Look at the Government, it's merely piling up debts and cutting positive programs.

Talk to small business people, they are surviving by downsizing.

Talk to employers, exorbitant health insurance and looming liability lawsuits are killing them off.

Talk to tradespeople, they will tell you of reduced benefits, fewer jobs and less securities.

Talk to trade unions, and you will hear about the diminishing influence of labor and the erosion of the minimum wage.

Talk to small farmers, and they will fill you in on their generationally owned farms now going down the drain of bankruptcy.

Talk to the real poor, they will inform you of mere subsistence and diminishing social programs.

A stone dropped in water causes ripples that travel outward. The stone causes this motion to happen.

I always regarded poverty as that stone.

Now I am beginning to see things differently. Could it be the ripples are coming inward instead? Could it be that it's the outer ripple that is the real problem?

History's major catastrophes seem to have happened that way. Hope this is not what is now happening to our country.

With every good wish,

Fr. Dan Madigan

182

Dear Friends:

I am now 58 years old. I have spent the last thirty plus years here in Sacramento City.

I find myself reminiscing a lot these days. Reminiscing as I officiate at the funerals of friends I have known over the past twenty or thirty years. Reminiscing as I marry people that I baptized as babies. Reminiscing as I baptize the little ones of the young folks I had in grade school.

Reminiscing when I visit Mercy McMahon Retirement Home and talk to my first pastor, Msgr. John Terwilliger. It was Fr. John who introduced me to the lovable, kind, generous and non-judgmental church that I know Christ wants to exist. It was Fr. John who also introduced me to some great restaurants like the Del Prado, Machiavelli's, Croce's, the Elbow Room, A.J. Bumps and D.O. Mills. Sadly all are now gone, only Al the Wops remains.

Reminiscing reaches its peak when **I visit the priests' plot at St. Mary's Cemetery.** As I walk from grave marker to grave marker, I cannot help but think of all those great men who have gone on ahead and the wonderful work they did.

However, I still have many friends who are alive and kicking as is evident from the work that is being accomplished at SFBS. You wonderful people make donations, put in countless hours of volunteer work, serve on boards and committees, help with fundraising, make presentations, serve as ambassadors of good will, and do all kinds of mentoring and hands-on work.

Now we invite you all to enjoy a dinner in Clarksburg on August 25. We also invite you to bring with you as guests whomever you wish.

Remember, Appreciation Day is a day specifically set aside by the SFBS Board, staff and me to thank you for being the great and wonderful people you are.

With every good wish,

Fr. Dan Madigan

OCTOBER 1996

Dear Friends:

Christ said He came down into this world to represent the poor. If you don't believe me please read
Luke 4:16-21.

In 1891 Pope Leo XIII wrote "RERUM NOVARUM"
In 1931 Pope Pius XI wrote "QUADRAGESIMO ANNO"
Both documents contain lots of honest talk about some very real issues. Together these two pieces of litera-
ture form the backbone for the Catholic Church's stance on social justice.

These documents minced no words when it came to talking about an honest day's work for an honest day's
pay. Neither do they run away from employer/employee relationships or the controversial issues of workers'
wages, health benefits and safety rights.

Recently, after an extensive search, I discovered copies of the above-mentioned documents in the basement
of a bookstore in San Francisco.

Since then I have imagined the Lord physically visiting us and watching His reaction to finding His powerful social documents in basements and His poor being bashed in newspaper headlines, magazine covers and
local billboards.

Friends, whether we like it or not, our country has:
- Ten million unemployed.
- Another ten million underemployed.
- And yet another ten million incapable of being employed.

And whether we like it or not, the simplistic cure that is being dished up to us by many of our political
people and by a sizeable segment of our church's hierarchical folks is simply not going to cut the mustard.

If Christ walked around our city today and observed the grandeur of our public buildings, the mag-
nificence of our freeway systems and the ostentatiousness of our churches, **and at the same time observed
the poverty** of many of our people, He would simply shake His head and say, *"When will they ever learn?
When will they ever learn?"*

With every good wish,

Fr. Dan Madigan

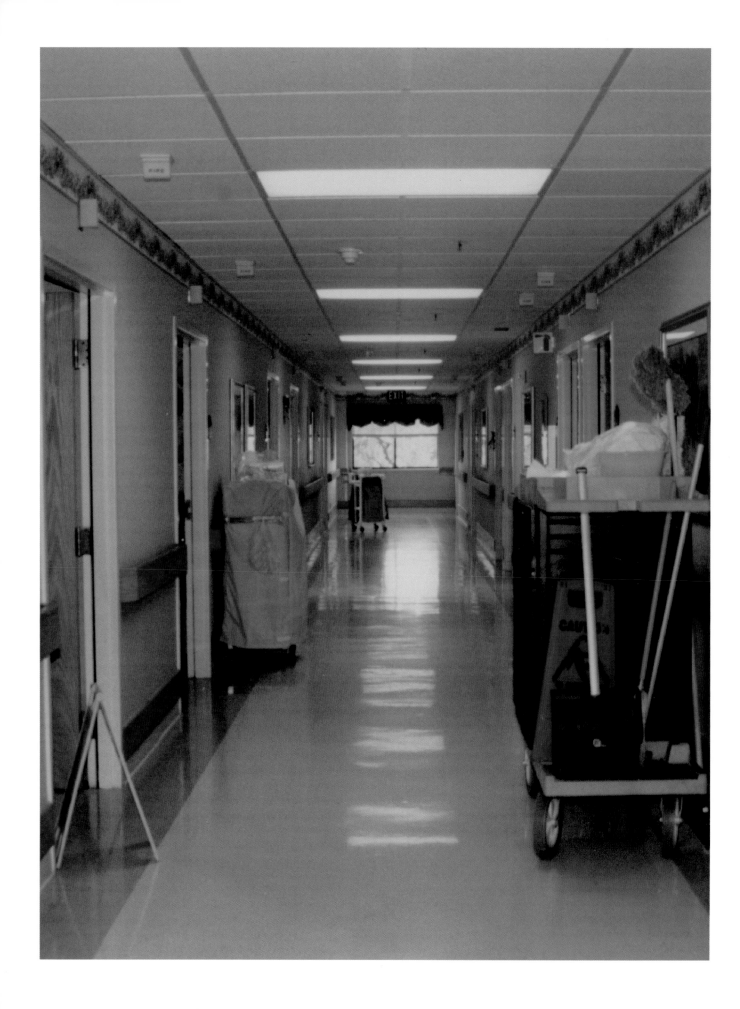

Dear Friends:

For over 30 years I have been visiting the hospitals of Sacramento. For over 30 years I have always found things pretty much the way I imagined they should be.

The evening of October 16 greatly changed my thinking. I visited one of our city's leading hospitals about 9:15 p.m. Found the main entrance section closed. Gained access through the emergency area. Traveled along some empty corridors. Took an elevator to the fifth floor where my patient supposedly was.

Upon arriving there I discovered the entire fifth floor totally abandoned of people. No patients. No nurses. No doctors. Nobody. After walking around several corridors and calling out for human contact I gave up and returned to the lobby. I explained my safari to some nurses. I asked if what I saw was real or was I hallucinating. They checked their computers and said my friend was truly on the 5th floor. One of them graciously took me up to see him. He was in an intensive care alcove area with a few other patients.

I drove home wondering what is coming over our medical system. **How could a whole floor of a modern hospital lie almost totally empty** while thousands of sick people are crying out for much needed medical attention? Expensive buildings I decided definitely are not the answer.

Then my mind wandered to a recent article in The Sacramento Bee. It told of Cardinal Mahoney's desire to build a $50 million dollar cathedral in Los Angeles. My mind still wandered on and I thought about the poor I see every day and what Saint John Chrysostom in his day said: *"If you saw someone in rags and stiff with cold and then did not give him clothing but set up golden columns in Christ's honor, would Christ not say that He was being made a fool of and insulted?"*

I retired that night wondering if I am somewhat out of step with the thinking of our country's government, nation's health care system and even my own beloved Church. Surely these great institutions cannot be wrong. Or could they?

It's Thanksgiving time again. We all have so many blessings to count. Please support us as you have in the past and be assured that your donation will be properly used by us for the betterment of our less fortunate sisters and brothers.

With every good wish,

Fr. Dan Madigan

DECEMBER 1996

Dear Friends:

I feel that Christmas is all about family. **All about those who are dear and close to us.**

I consider myself one of the luckiest men on earth. Over 30 years of living in Sacramento has provided me with an enormous family. Food Bank folks from all walks of life, staff, volunteers, donors, media folks and the dear people who come for a little help.

I am also blessed with parishioners present and past, Rotarians, Senior Gleaners, Over the Hill Gang and the list goes on and on.

Recently a group of my fellow priests decided to jump on board SFBS and join me in a more hands-on way. These men will advise our already existing board in the making of needed decisions necessary for daily operations and long range planning.

The priests are:

Fr. Simon Twomey	*Pastor, Presentation Parish, Sacramento*
Fr. Michael Carroll	*Mercy Hospital Hospice Chaplain*
Msgr. James Church	*Pastor, St. Philomene Parish, Sacramento*
Fr. Nicholas Duggan	*Pastor, St. Paul Parish, Sacramento*
Fr. John Healy	*Mercy General Hospital Chaplain*
Fr. Daniel Looney	*Pastor, St. James Parish, Davis*
Fr. Patrick McGrath	*Pastor, St. Joseph Parish, Rio Vista*

I consider the decision that these men have made to join us in serving the poor through SFBS to be the most wonderful Christmas gift I could possibly receive.

May the good Lord bless you and your loved ones during this beautiful season we are about to celebrate. May He also bless you for the great kindness you continue to show the less fortunate among us.

With every good wish,

Fr. Dan Madigan

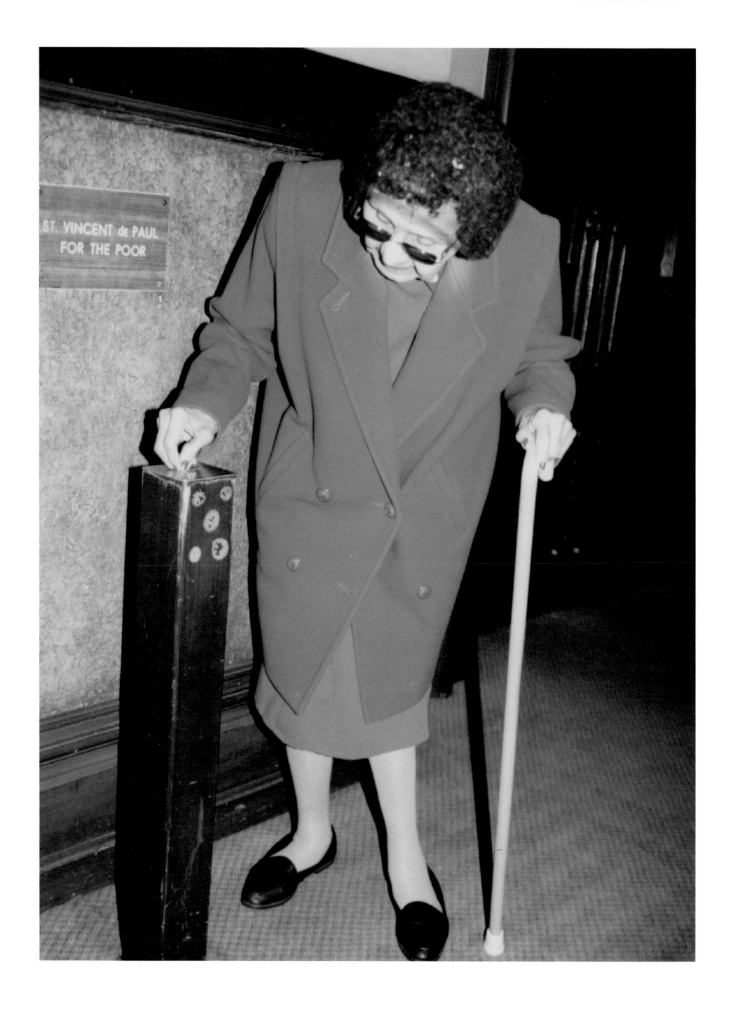

190

Dear Friends:

On behalf of the poor of Sacramento County I want to express my deepest gratitude to each and every one of you who have supported our Food Bank over the holiday periods of Thanksgiving and Christmas.

Our thanks go out not alone to individuals but to churches, synagogues, clubs, organizations, schools, government agencies, financial institutions, businesses, newspaper and TV stations.

Sacramentans, please remember that while your generosity has been overwhelming during these past several weeks, I must remind you that hunger and need are year-round problems.

People have a tendency to associate hunger with cold weather. However, there are just as many people in line on a 100-plus day in August as there are on a cold wet day in January.

To those of you who have grasped the year-round need and support us on an ongoing basis, I want to truly recognize your goodness. To everyone else, no matter how often you donate, no matter how big, no matter how small, no matter how seldom, your goodness to us is deeply, deeply appreciated.

Our Lord admired the woman who dropped the penny in the box. We here at SFBS do the same.

May 1997 bring you and yours much health and lots and lots of happiness. May God truly bless you with deep inner peace each day of your life.

With every good wish,

Fr. Dan Madigan

192

Dear Friends:

Ralph Waldo Emerson said: *"Common sense is as rare as genius."*

His statement certainly applies to our government. Look at the mess in which the welfare system exists.

The Federal folks tell the States that they must have twenty-five percent of welfare recipients in the work force by October and fifty percent of welfare recipients working within five years. Furthermore, all welfare recipients will be limited to a lifetime span of five years on welfare aid.

I totally agree that work and self-sufficiency are the answer, but I disagree that this utopia of everyone having a job can be achieved by the mere passing of laws.

Thirty years of ringside sitting with the poor has shown me that poverty is a very complex problem. Over these thirty years I have discovered that many poor people have multitudinous problems and most welfare recipients are in dire need of tender coaching from highly motivated volunteers.

Government agencies are unable to produce the calibre of teachers I feel are essential to uplift and guide the poor people I know.

However, what baffles me most is why the government refuses to study and support agencies like ours which have a proven record of positive accomplishments? Maybe someday it will.

In the meantime, SFBS will continue to do what it has been doing these past 21 years, **working together** with you wonderful people and accomplishing much good for the poor of the Sacramento community.

With every good wish,

Fr. Dan Madigan

Dear Friends:

Henry Ford said, *"Most people spend more time and energy going around problems than trying to solve them."*

Here at SFBS we try and tackle problems head on. Our goal is not to be the voice of conservatism, not the voice of liberalism, but the voice of sanity and credibility.

Daily we see:
- *Soaring divorce rates*
- *Fatherless homes*
- *Thirteen-year-old children having babies*
- *Homeless families*
- *A pandemic of sexually transmitted diseases*
- *Sociopathic children*
- *Violence that makes many people prisoners in their own homes*

However, the majority we daily see are:
- *The working poor*
- *Struggling people who are endowed with a large dose of human goodness but need help with self-reliance, determination and resourcefulness*

We try and expose all people to the thinking of Mary Pickford: *"Failure isn't falling down, it's staying down."*

We explain to struggling people they will never reach the top if they are constantly preoccupied with problems. **We try and help them** flip over the coin and see the other side and thus become consumed with life's opportunities. We constantly strive to teach them self-betterment through self-empowerment.

Dear readers, you are right in the trenches with us through your monetary contributions and volunteer hours. Please remember that together we are making a huge difference in the lives of many of Sacramento's poor.

With every good wish,

Fr. Dan Madigan

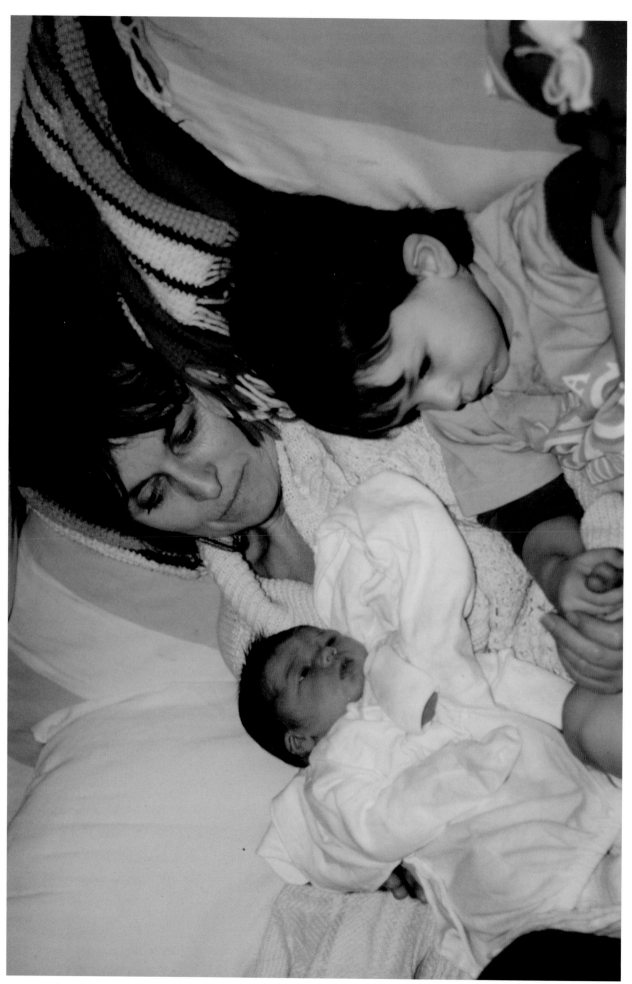

196

Dear Friends:

Recently, Ann Bancroft and I joined forces in putting together a book titled "Many Hands, Many Miracles." This book was published by Notre Dame Press and some copies are still available through the Food Bank.

Here is what the Sacramento Bee said in its editorial December 16, 1996:

In 1964, a newly ordained Irish-born priest, Dan Madigan, was dispatched by the Roman Catholic Church to a poor parish in an exotic-sounding place called Del Paso Heights. For six years, Madigan happily ministered to the poor in the ramshackle semirural neighborhood north of Sacramento.

Then in 1970 he was 'promoted' to the Fabulous 40's, a wealthy parish in east Sacramento, former home to Gov. Ronald Reagan and other rich local movers and shakers. Adrift amid the mansions, Madigan felt useless and welcomed. In fact, he begged for a transfer six years later to Oak Park, another poor, but this time inner-city neighborhood.

As 'Many Hands, Many Miracles,' a new book by Madigan and local Associated Press reporter and volunteer Ann Bancroft, explains, Madigan's sojourn among the haves and the have-nots served its purpose. It gave Madigan the contacts he needed to build Sacramento Food Bank Services, one of the largest and most successful charities in Sacramento County.

*Founded by Madigan 20 years ago, SFBS is a $10 million annual enterprise today. It does more than just feed the poor; **it clothes and shelters them**, and, perhaps most important, it helps repair and renew broken lives. Poor mothers are given formula and diapers but also taught how to raise healthy and happy children. The homeless are not just taken off the streets but given guidance on how to get and keep jobs, budget their money and manage their households. The illiterate are taught to read.*

His work is not without controversy. The poor can be troublesome and even dangerous neighbors. As the number of homeless rise, impacted communities view charities with increasing hostility. Madigan has not escaped the wrath.

Nonetheless, he remains an important asset. The poor are not the only ones he serves. SFBS provides an opportunity to the thousands in this community who fervently want to reach out to their less fortunate neighbors to do so. Father Madigan has brought those two worlds together in a way that benefits both and enriches the city at the same time.

While I want to thank you, Sacramento Bee, for mentioning our book, I especially want to say how much I admire what you do for Sacramento's poor.

With every good wish,

Fr. Dan Madigan

Dear Friends:

Our television reports recently told us that **more U.S. people will do air travel this year** than ever before. The TV people said, *"It's because our economy is so good."*

At the same time our local newspaper painted a different picture. It explained how City Manager Bill Edgar and County Executive Bob Thomas had to face big budget cuts because of the lack of adequate income.

How we see life depends on the perch on which we sit. If our situation is good, then we believe everyone else's is also.

No so from my perch. It looks like we are nose-diving.

Minimum wage just doesn't cut it any more. A breadwinner can't raise a family on a Subway or Burger King or Taco Bell salary. Yet many parents are trying to do just that, raise their kids on a combination of minimum wage income and food locker handouts.

Daily I ask myself if the lack of money is the root cause of most of our problems, and if a change in economics would indeed set people on a much different kind of road.

The answer, I believe, is "M & M's".
Poor people need "MORE MONEY AND MORE MENTORING".

Living in Clarksburg this past winter taught me the value of the levee. Without those river banks our area would have been a swamp.

Like the river levees, the levees of family life have to be maintained and repaired. Togetherness, accountability, determination, courage and self-esteem protect the family and these values must return to bolster the family levees.

Shattered families need the help of dedicated folks like you. You are their only hope. Please don't turn your back on them. Join us in helping them.

With every good wish,

Fr. Dan Madigan

Dear Friends:

Earlier this year, my friend, Richard White, invited me to visit his hometown of New York. It was a wonderful experience. Here are a few of my thoughts.

I was born in Shanagolden, County Limerick, Ireland.

My family continues to live in the house where my Great-grandfather, Grandfather, Father and I were born.

My folks still wile away those long winter evenings with friends and neighbors in front of an ever-present blazing fire.

Sitting by that fireside as a child I can recall the conversations drifting off to distant places where none of the adults had ever been, but, through the osmosis of homecoming Yanks, we felt acquainted with places like Manhattan, the Bronx, Staten Island and Brooklyn.

Richard took me to see all these places that I once dreamed I would one day see.

In its subways I felt the pulse of this great metropolis. Under its streets I rubbed shoulders with a sprinkling of its seven million people, people from every country, race and culture.

In my early childhood, next to the Mother of God and my own mom, stood Lady Liberty. Visiting her at her home was a sacred experience. *"Give me your poor, your tired, your huddled masses yearning to breathe free",* she said. I stood there and thanked God for the privilege of being one of her children.

Next I visited Ellis Island. I browsed around its Great Hall. I visualized the hardships and sacrifices of the teeming multitudes waiting to be processed. Truly this is hallowed ground, a portal of hope for those accepted, and an isle of tears for those deported.

Later I went a quarter of a mile up into the air to the top of the Empire State Building. The view from its 102nd floor observatory was so stupendous that I had no trouble believing that within a year four million people would come up to see what I was now looking at.

It's said that New York belongs to everyone. I can attest to that. While there I had the opportunity to speak to people as diverse as John Cardinal O'Connor, of New York Archdiocese, Frank McCourt, author of Angela's Ashes, Jerry Adams, Sinn Fein's leader, and Soledad O'Brien of NBC News.

I left New York vowing to return. The city's lack of prejudice won my heart. Acceptance seemed to flow to us both from the haves and the have-nots. The fact that New York spends more on social services than any other major city in the United States sat well with me.

Yes, I loved New York. It seemed to have lots of room for the unfettered mind.

With every good wish,

Fr. Dan Madigan

Dear Friends:

I really admire people who can put a wealth of knowledge into a simple phrase.

Henry Ford was good at it. He said, ***"Most people spend more time and energy going around problems than trying to solve them."***

One of the first things I learned in mathematics was that the shortest distance between point A and point B is a straight line.

However, today's society seems to know very little about this basic gem of wisdom.

Many in our legal system refuse to adhere to common sense, as do many in government, schools, health and church fields.

So, consequently, non-involvement, avoidance of issues and overall confusion has become the king of the forest.

This madness just cannot continue. People have to put a stop to it. Common sense, ethical behavior and old time spirituality have to return to daily living.

Mary Pickford said, *"Failure isn't falling down, it's staying down."*

You and I have to get up and get going.

Our Food Bank here is making a big difference.

If you can, please send us a contribution this month. Believe me we are very much in need of it.

With every good wish,

Fr. Dan Madigan

Dear Friends:

In my opinion, overcoming our country's social ills, poverty, crime and dysfunctional living, is not at all beyond our capacity.

However, overcoming unjust systems, be they in business, government or church, is something I feel is not as easily attainable.

I just finished watching the movie "Cool Hand Luke." Luke's only crime was non-conformity.

Luke refused to be a patsy to his cruel masters, so they killed him for not communicating with them in the manner they desired.

Luke reminds me of Jesus Christ.

The Good Lord Himself paid a big price for speaking out.

Officialdom likes conformity. Authoritarian institutions often defend their status quo even if it entails resorting to veiled injustice.

This is not correct behavior. Right is right and wrong is wrong no matter how we paint it.

The Bible tells us to say "yes" when we mean yes, and "no" when we mean no.

So let's pray that the old days of honesty, integrity and **handshake commitments** will return again.

With every good wish,

Fr. Dan Madigan

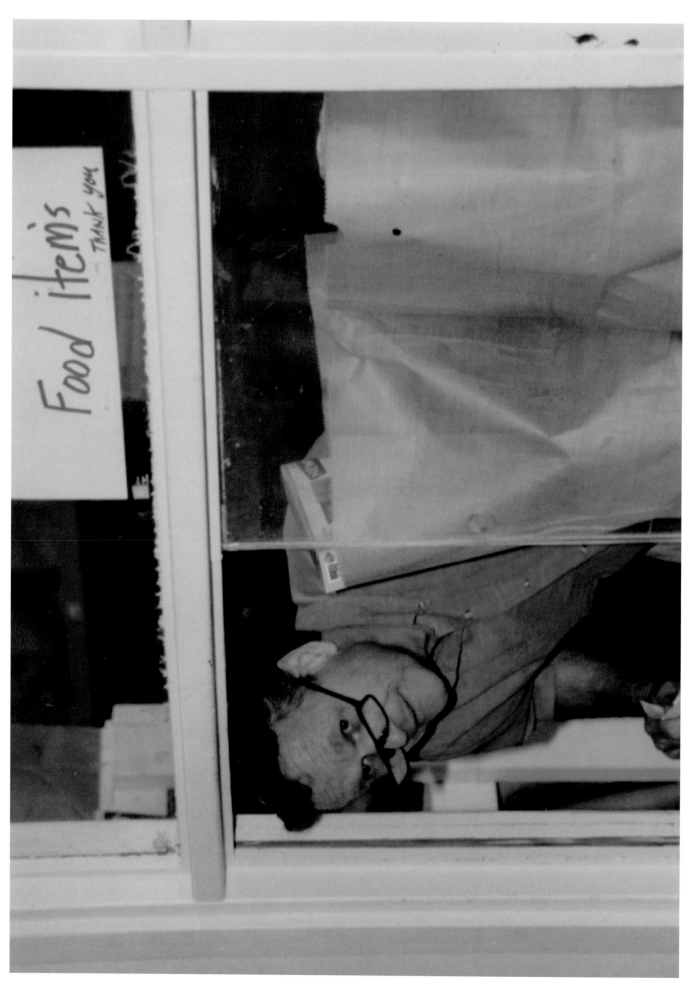

Dear Friends:

Running an agency of our magnitude is no small undertaking. Daily we cope with ongoing variables such as:

- The number of people who come to us for help
- The corps of volunteers who show up to work
- The amount of food and goods we glean
- The donations that arrive in the mail

For the past 21 years I have become used to daily walking the high wire and knowing how easy it is to topple at any given moment. However, through the grace of God, we have never once had to close our doors or cut back on our services.

Over the years I have gone to church and prayed to God about having to daily walk the razor's edge of financial inadequacy. On my knees I have talked to many of the great folks whom I have buried and then and there asked them to intercede to God for us.

What I do works because the answer that always arrives back is: DON'T JUST BELIEVE IN MIRACLES, RELY ON THEM.

And so we have.

And for 21 years Sacramentans have stood by us.

Good folks, you are the instruments God uses to make all our great work happen. With God as our captain, you on our team and my staff as the ethical hard-working coaches they are, we will again **do as good a job this Christmas** as we have in the past ones.

Please, please remember, no donation to us is too small.

May God truly bless you this Holy Christmas Season.

With every good wish,

Fr. Dan Madigan

JANUARY 1998

Dear Friends:

Recently I was asked by an official Church representative if my work at the Food Bank was *purely secular.* My reply was *"definitely not."*

For many people religion seems confined to church buildings and to the liturgies, prayers, hymns and Bible readings that take place therein.

Many people also reduce compassionate servanthood of the poor to mere humanitarian effort and to optional involvement.

Optional involvement is not what I read in the Scriptures. And neither is it the way that many of the saints saw it. Believe me, many of these great people put their lives on the line for the social message of the Gospel.

On December 8, 1992, we here at SFBS opened up our Mother/Baby Program. From the very beginning we handed out absolutely free of charge:

- Formula and baby food
- Baby care Items
- Individual emotional support
- Parental mentoring
- Family education classes
- Immunization

Our Mother/Baby Program is in ongoing need of:

Volunteers	–A couple of hours a week or even a couple of hours a month
Baby food	–formula, cereal, canned juice
Baby care items	–diapers, bedding, powder, soap, pacifiers, carryalls
Mentors	–people with warm hearts and common sense
Family education classes	–people willing to make presentations on baby care, self-esteem, money management, food preparation, grooming, etc.

We deliberately chose December 8, the birthday of the good Lord's Mom, to start up this program, and she has truly blessed us because in the past year of 1997 we saw 24,000 babies and gave them 77,000 food products, 27,000 hygiene items and 320,000 diapers.

Friends, I want to thank you for your ongoing support of our programs. Remember we do what we do because you are **a part of our team.**

May God bless you and watch over you in this New Year of ours.

With every good wish,

Fr. Dan Madigan

217

Dear Friends:

A Glorious Epic, Gigantic, Spectacular, Awesome are the newspaper phrases used to describe the move "Titanic." I went to see the show and must say it is extravaganza at its best.

However, for thought provoking ideas, I had to turn to a book. And I found some very challenging thoughts in a volume titled ***"Jesus CEO"***. It is a national bestseller, written by Laurie Beth Jones and published by Hyperion.

I was so impressed with this book I sent a copy to Bishop William Weigand. I mentioned to him that I wish I had the privilege of reading it some 30 years ago. I also suggested he invite its author to come and make a presentation to us priests.

I have never met Laurie Beth Jones. I am mentioning her book because I consider it *"good stuff"*. Good stuff deserves reading. She certainly knows all about leadership and how it's best utilized.

We at SFBS demand a high standard of leadership from our program directors. All are expected to:

- Clearly define in writing their program's goals and their planned strategy for turning these goals into reality.
- Inspire, lead, motivate and cement their volunteers into an organized army to accomplish their goals.
- Surround themselves with a highly competent board which assists them with their program's ongoing strategy formation, implementation and evaluation.

Friends, we try to do things right. We constantly work on our overall mission, philosophy and strategy.

Please come volunteer with us. We will find a slot to fit your time schedule and desires.

With every good wish,

Fr. Dan Madigan

Dear Friends:

All of us are scared of *pain, fear, loneliness and powerlessness.*

Yet Richard Cardinal Cushing says trouble is the best thing that ever happens to us.

More people, he says, have been made great by crosses than by crowns.

More people have been blessed by hardships than through prosperity.

Cushing's knowledge comes from both family background and deep insight into Christ's Beatitudes.

Christ warns us that wealth and power, because of their innate props, can easily lead us into the dangerous fields of arrogance, righteousness and pomposity.

Whereas pain and want, with their absence of props, usually strips one down to honesty, humility and kindness.

Bernard Shulman, an esteemed Chicago psychiatrist, says, *"People are more like dogs than cats".*

Cats can spend countless hours in solitude, but not dogs that constantly seek companionship.

We humans cannot go it alone either. **We need each other.**

So now with the penitential days of the Lenten Season upon us, let's reach out more to unfortunate people and help them the best way we can.

May the good Lord bless each and every one of you.

With every good wish,

Fr. Dan Madigan

Dear Friends:

Christ's parables are laden with deep compassion.

It's because of them I became a priest.

The Prodigal Son, The Lost Sheep, The Good Samaritan, appealed to me in a special way.

The Unforgiving Servant, The Publican and the Pharisee, The Rich Man and Lazarus showed me what's important and what's not important in life.

Christ's interaction with the Ten Lepers, Mary Magdalen, The Thief on the Cross, and The Apostles Washing of Feet, carries much wisdom for daily meditation.

Officialdom sat poorly with Christ. He found this authoritarian group bereft of compassion, and He was not afraid to tell them so.

Today I feel this severity of old may very well be returning. I notice its head sticking up in some of our great fields such as medicine, education, law and even the Church.

Recently El Nino threw beautiful homes into the ocean. Lack of compassion can as easily throw beautiful people over the cliff if we allow it to happen, but we cannot.

Christ spent much time showing us how to respect each other. How to uplift each other. We cannot just walk away and ignore His compassionate approach and His expectations of us to follow His way.

Take care, good folks. By the way, our funds are rather low at the moment. If you can help, please do.

With every good wish,

Fr. Dan Madigan

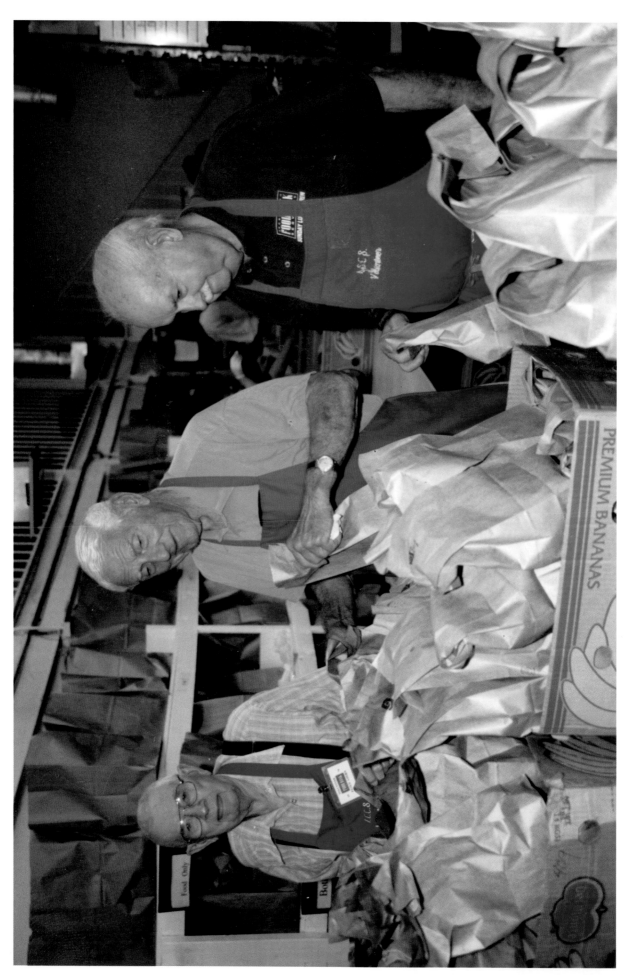

Dear Friends:

I was born in 1938. Bridie, my sister, in 1924.

While I was in the cradle, Bridie was off to boarding school.

Upon my entering high school, Bridie graduated as a radiographer.

As I entered the seminary, Bridie married.

And as I became a pastor, she died.

Bridie lived in Perth, Western Australia. She died of cancer.

Apart from her husband and four children, the greatest legacy my beloved sister left me was a statement made by one of her friends, *"There was never a lame duck that landed in Perth that your sister did not take under her wing".*

What a noble epitaph.

It was because of Bridie's life that I was able to say in one of my recent newsletters: *"It is not the amount of years we spend between the cradle and the grave that matters. It's the way we live them. It's the amount of good we squeeze into them. The things we do that better and brighten the lives of others that makes the big difference".*

Life is all about compassion. If we possess it we have everything. If we lack it we are truly sad and lost people.

Now, my friends, if you are in a position to send a donation this month, be assured we need it.

In closing my wish for you is that the good Lord will truly bless you and yours.

With every good wish,

Fr. Dan Madigan

JULY 1998

Dear Friends:

Sacramento Food Bank Services is a 22-year-old comprehensive social service agency.

I am its founder. I work with its mission, vision, public relations and fundraising. I do its correspondence.

I make my monthly newsletters educational and at the same time politely ask for volunteer help and monetary donations.

This letter is different. This letter is for *prayer.*

Let me begin by saying that SFBS is an immensely complicated piece of machinery. Daily it works with a plethora of variables: seven hundred volunteers, ninety-five percent community raised budget, a horde of clients with multitudinous problems, and a philosophy of service almost synonymous with Utopia.

There is an old Latin aphorism *"Fortune favors the Bold".* This maxim worked well for us six years ago when we hired the brightest and best professional we could find. **Leslie Elgood** came to us with the zeal of a missioner, the integrity of a saint and the stamina of Mother Teresa.

Just as Our Lord had to contend with the storm on the Sea of Galilee, so had Leslie with some floundering days at SFBS. Because of her managerial skill, we now have a very smooth running agency that is accomplishing an enormous amount of good.

However, Leslie is leaving us on July 23. She has accepted the position of Director of Major Gifts and Planned Giving for the University of New Mexico in Albuquerque.

Please pray that we get a dynamo of a person to replace her, someone who dearly loves the poor, is endowed with a huge amount of common sense, and who has uncompromising endurance. Someone who is well versed in management, and has the skill to handle a high level of stress.

So now, my Food Bank friends, you see why I plead for your prayers. Please do not forget this agency which you love and believe in when you talk with Almighty God.

With every good wish,

Fr. Dan Madigan

Dear Friends:

Thirty years of working with the poor has shown me that great things happen when good people put their shoulder to the wheel.

The church pew people need the poor. The poor need the folks from the church pew.

George Gallup says it takes the raw material of life - despair, uncertainty, apprehension, pain - to bring people to God.

If you have not experienced emotional, psychological or physical pain in life come pay us a visit.

Stay with us for a while and you will see some horrible situations. Work with us and you will become more empathetic, more spiritual, and closer to God than you have ever been.

When I was a youngster every Irish village had four revered people: the priest, the doctor, the teacher, and the civic guard.

These people stood for what was right. All the time.

Villagers held them in great esteem. Salt of the earth they were, and all knew it.

Now look at what has happened. The pulley has fallen into the well.

Priests have become administrators. Doctors have become pawns of HMO's. Civic guards have turned into armed police. Teachers scurry from dysfunctional classrooms. The poor are corralled in the ghettos of our cities.

Separation of Church and State is a good thing I guess, but confining religion to church buildings is not.

Church people have what it takes to turn irresponsible teenagers into conscientious youngsters. Spiritual folks can gently change dysfunctional women into competent moms. People with high ethical standards can convince young males to become responsible fathers.

Yes integrity, decency and sensitivity can overcome the topsy-turvy world of the inner-city. No good parent wants his or her kids to be unnurtured, undisciplined, unfed, unwashed and unmedicated. They just need to be shown that there is another road open to them and that it is reachable.

With every good wish,

Fr. Dan Madigan

Dear Friends:

My dad was gentle, kind, humorous, self-educated and steeped in integrity.

Dad's long gone on to his Creator but I still carry around with me many of his simple sayings, *"Don't ever throw water on a drowning rat"* he would tell us. On the farm a rat was a filthy disease carrier. A drowning rat was one in deep trouble, yet my dad said don't add to his misfortune. Leave him alone. He has enough problems.

The chickens in the coop taught me the opposite lesson. These little birds were all great friends until one of them accidentally got its skin torn in the wire of the cage. At the first sight of blood all its family descended upon it like vampires and pecked it to death. No mercy shown, just plain cruelty.

Our Lord gave us many cornerstones to build upon. He let us know He had no time for pomposity, arrogance or judgmental behavior. He constantly preached compassion and tolerance. He said, ***"Let the person who is without sin cast the first stone"***.

There is no denying that present society has enormous mindboggling problems. It's frightening to watch the evening news. The muddy lake of life is full of drowning people.

We at SFBS work with these folks. We constantly ask ourselves, why are they in there? Are they just jumping in? Or is someone throwing them in? Or are they actually born in this swamp?

These are big, big questions. However, they are totally necessary questions, because if we don't make inroads with the "whys" we certainly will not find any solutions.

May God bless you for being a player on our team.

With every good wish,

Fr. Dan Madigan

Dear Friends:

Apart from my work with SFBS I am also pastor of St. Joseph's in Clarksburg.

St. Joseph's is a quaint little brick church. It is located in Yolo County on the banks of the Sacramento River. It's directly across the river from the town of Freeport. It sits in a parklike setting of shrubbery, trees and lawns. It is totally surrounded by hundreds of acres of grape fields. It's about a fifteen minute drive from Sacramento.

Life is rural at St. Joseph's. We have our own well, our own septic system, and because we often lose electrical power we have our own generator. Rural living is no stranger to me. In fact, I am very much in love with the life style it offers.

The cast iron pump in the photo supplied us "Madigans" with water when I was a youngster. The onslaught of Irish rural electrification in the late '40's outmoded this little instrument. Nostalgia helped me save it from the briar patch and haul it across the Atlantic to my home here in Clarksburg. This cast iron piece of metal is precious to me. For years it brought my family life sustaining water from under the earth. All we had to do was pump,

"Priming the pump" is a phrase you may not be familiar with. While a hand pump is working all is fine, but when it is allowed to lay idle its inners dry up and so will not work again without adding some water to it. This is called *"priming."*

In a book called "Growing Into Light," Max Long writes about a leathery old Westerner who called himself Desert Pete. Living out in the sun-beaten country where water is so very precious, Desert Pete wrote a note, put it in a baking powder can and wired it to an old pump. Here is what he wrote:

> *Under the white rock I buried a bottle of water, out of the sun,*
> *cork end up. There's enough water in it to prime this pump,*
> *but not if you drink some first. Pour about one fourth, and let*
> *her soak to wet the leather. Then pour the rest medium fast*
> *and pump. You'll git water. The well has never run dry.*
> *Have faith. When you git watered up, fill the bottle and put it*
> *back like you found it for the next feller.*

To me SFBS is like that hand pump. As the pump has access to the water so has SFBS to food, clothing, housing, baby care items, mentors and educators.

However, without *primer* (cash contributions) and *pumpers* (volunteers) we would go nowhere. But with the help of primer and pumpers we really work miracles.

This month please be kind to us as you always have.

With every good wish,

Fr. Dan.

Fr. Dan Madigan

234

Dear Friends:

The months of November and December are at our doorstep. Twenty-two years of experience have proven to me that these are the giving months.

There are three types of giving: **Self-giving. Forgiving. Thanksgiving.**

<u>Self-giving</u> is explained by Winston Churchill when he says, *"We make a living by what we get, we make a life by what we give."*

<u>Forgiving</u> is well summed up by Alton Paton when he says, *"When a deep injury is done to us we never recover until we forgive."*

<u>Thanksgiving</u> is so important that we Americans specifically lay aside one day a year to celebrate it. As that day approaches let each one of us:

- Count our blessings instead of our crosses.
- Count our gains instead of our losses.
- Count our joys instead of our woes.
- Count our friends instead of our foes.
- Count our smiles instead of our tears.
- Count our courage instead of our fears.
- Count our full years instead of our lean.
- Count our kind deeds instead of our mean.
- Count our health instead of our wealth.
- Count on God instead of ourselves.

SFBS exists because of you and thousands of generous people like you.

You believe in what we do and you support us.

With every good wish,

Fr. Dan Madigan

December 1998

Dear Friends:

It's impossible to hide starvation. It's difficult to hide malnutrition. But it's easy to hide hunger. That's what many Sacramentans do. **They hide their poverty, and come to the Food Bank as a last resort.**

Daily we see what deprivation does to families:
- It disintegrates them.
- It wears away their morale.
- It destroys their physical health.
- It shatters their emotional well-being.
- It categorizes them as dysfunctional.
- It saddles them as societal failures.

I pray I will see the day when our country will stand up and say:
- We now have enough studies, commissions and reports.
- Poverty in our country is unacceptable.
- Illiteracy among our people is unacceptable.
- Homelessness is unacceptable.

I also pray I will see the day when church-going folks will get out of their pews:
- To feed, clothe, and house people.
- To befriend, mentor, and counsel them.
- To walk with them hand-in-hand.
- To journey with them from the slavery of persistent poverty.
- To the freedom of attainable self-actualization.

We all see life from the tunnel we live in, or from the mountain top on which we reside, or from the platform upon which we daily stand. Here is what SFBS has seen in the last 20 years:

In 1977 we fed   9,000 people
In 1987 we fed 253,000 people
In 1997 we fed 495,000 people

St. John Chrysostom said, *"The rich man is not one who is in possession of much, but one who gives much"*.

In the same way it follows that the rich church is not the one which builds grand buildings but the one which truly cares for people.

With every good wish,

Fr. Dan Madigan

Dear Friends:

"Zero Tolerance" was one of the buzz phrases of 1998.

It was readily on the tongues of aspiring politicians, hard-nosed correctional people, tough school administrators and righteous talk show hosts.

Many people liked it. Many of us did not.

Its guarantee to solve the problems of our topsy-turvy world is, to say the least, naïve.

Violence begets violence.

The Lord knew that.

That's why **He advocated deep compassion, total tolerance and a great gentleness.**

At SFBS we endorse the spoonful of honey not the barrel of vinegar.

Through gentle volunteer mentoring we encourage those who come to us for help to embrace lofty aspirations and practical accountability.

SFBS is far from being wishy-washy. We opt for the "Beatitudes of Christ" not "Zero Tolerance" thinking.

SFBS is financed by Sacramentans (6900 donors)
SFBS work force is all Sacramentans (700 volunteers)
The good accomplished by SFBS is done by the city's citizenry for the city's poor.

And you, kind-hearted, supporter-donor-volunteer-participant, no matter what your race, color, religious affiliation in life is, you are truly a member of our SFBS family.

Thank you for your tremendous kindness to the Food Bank over the year of 1998. Hope that your health and your income allow you to be as kind to us in this year of 1999.

With every good wish,

Fr. Dan Madigan

240

Dear Friends:

Even though it's around twenty years ago, I vividly remember a conversation I had with Fr. Joe Ternullo as we ate our evening dinner at Immaculate Conception Rectory in Oak Park.

Fr. Joe told me his dad, Sam, had purchased a new automobile at an excellent price. Joe went on to say that when the cost was sealed in concrete, his dad paid in cash. This action of his dad infuriated the salesman.

That evening's conversation was a milestone in my life. Until then I thought that cash in hand was the greatest way of leveraging a bargain. Now I was being introduced to the new world of finance with loan payments and the stringent interest that accompanied them.

Last year U.S. households spent seventy billion dollars in interest charges and fees.

Three thousand credit card transactions a second were processed during the Holiday Season of Thanksgiving and Christmas, and this was on Visa cards alone.

In 1983 twenty percent of poor families had credit. In 1995 forty percent did.

Times have not changed since the Irish Molly Maguire coal miners fought their bosses and tried winning back their lives that were owned by the company store. The same battle needs to be fought again. Today, because of plastic credit cards, many people still owe their souls to the company store.

Credit card debt has risen 23.5 percent in just over a year and is growing far faster than all other types of borrowing, including home mortgages and auto loans.

Like the cunning spider the plastic card industry is pulling the poor into the web of no escape.

SFBS intends doing something about this. We would like to start by gathering together a cadre of people who believe as we do. If you are one of those folks who are willing to put your shoulder to the wheel to help fight this wrong, please give Peter Berghuis or me a call.

The ensnared poor need our help. So many are presently in the quicksand and going under fast.

May the good Lord bless you for your kindness and goodness to SFBS.

With every good wish,

Fr. Dan Madigan

Dear Friends:

The uplifting of people is the work of Sacramento Food Bank Services. Shackles, manacles, fetters are items we abhor. That's why in my last month's newsletter I spoke of the galling chain of credit card entrapment.

Peter Berghuis, our Executive Director, and I received several replies to my appeal for input and help. Some told us how credit cards had destroyed members of their family. A friend's letter advised me to abandon this impossible task as I would be merely wasting my time fighting against this mountain of wrong.

Now while I have the deepest respect by my learned friend, I feel I must instead adhere to the sage advice of Charles F. Kettering, *"Nothing ever built arose to touch the skies unless some man dreamed that it should, some man believed that it could, and some man willed that it must."*

Peter Berghuis will be heading up this effort. Peter is six foot nine inches tall, and when he puts his shoulder to a wheel, even though that wheel be a millstone, it moves a little.

St. Patrick's Day is almost upon us. I am including in this letter an article titled "How Dagger John Saved New York's Irish". Dagger John was Bishop John Joseph Hughes of New York. The following article written by William J. Stern was published in the Wall Street Journal on March 17, 1997.

"We are not the first generation puzzled by what to do about the underclass. One hundred and fifty years ago, Manhattan's tens of thousands of Irish seemed mired in poverty and ignorance, destroying themselves through drink, idleness, violence, crime and illegitimacy. Yet within a generation, New York's Irish had flooded into the American mainstream. No job-training program or welfare system brought about so sweeping a change. How Bishop John Joseph Hughes – "more a Roman gladiator than a devout follower of the meek founder of Christianity," according to a newspaper reporter of his time – helped accomplish this revolution in values can teach us volumes about our own social problems.

An Irish immigrant who began his life in America as a gardener, Hughes was consecrated bishop of New York on Jan. 7, 1838. Nicknamed Dagger John for his combativeness, he immediately stirred up a war over the Public School Society, demanding state aid for Catholic schools, just as the state had funded denominational schools before 1826. The outcome pleased no one. The Maclay Bill of 1842 barred all religious instruction from public schools and provided no state money to parochial schools. Hughes then threw his energies into building a Catholic school system that emphasized a faith-based code of conduct and respect for teachers and fellow students. Parents were required to attend meetings with teachers and to help maintain the schools.

The Great Irish Famine struck in 1845 bringing Hughes his greatest challenge. Two million Irish fled to the U.S. in the following 15 years, most arrived at New York, where they settled into appalling living conditions. Shanties sprang up in alleys. Without running water, sewage piled up in backyard privies; rats and cholera reigned. Hughes's flock formed an underclass in which every social pathology flourished. The response from native born Americans fierce anti-immigrant sentiment asserting the genetic inferiority of the Irish.

An estimated 50,000 Irish prostitutes worked the city in 1850, and the Five Points neighborhood in Manhattan's "Bloody Sixth" Ward alone had 17 brothels. Illegitimacy soared; tens of thousands of abandoned Irish kids roamed the city's streets. Violent Irish gangs fought each other and anti-Catholic "nativists," but primarily they robbed houses and small businesses. More than half the people arrested in

New York in the 1840's and 1850's were Irish; police vans were dubbed "paddy wagons" and episodes of mob violence in the streets were called "donnybrooks," after the Irish town. The death rate among Irish families in New York in the 1850's was 21%, while among non-Irish it was 3%.

In response to such inner-city blight, Hughes began a mission of urban evangelization aimed at giving the immigrants a faith-based system of personal responsibility. Sex outside marriage was sinful, no exceptions. Since alcohol was such a major problem for his flock, Hughes – though no teetotaler himself – promoted the formation of a Catholic abstinence society. In 1849 he accompanied the famous Irish Capuchin Father Theobald Mathew, the "apostle of temperance," as he gave his abstinence pledge to 20,000 New Yorkers.

Faced with as many as 60,000 Irish children wandering the city, Hughes encouraged the formation of the Society for the Protection of Destitute Catholic Children, known as the Catholic Protectory. The Protectory purchased a 114-acre farm near Westchester, NY; its head, Levi Ives, wrote that "by proper religious instruction and the teaching of useful trades (the Protectory) could raise the children above their slum environment." Hughes encouraged the formation of church societies to help people deal with personal, family and neighborhood problems. He also helped form the Irish Emigrant Society to get jobs for his flock. The nuns in his diocese became employment agents for Irish domestics: Rich families knew that a maid or cook the nuns recommended would be honest and reliable. The nuns encouraged Irish women to run boarding houses for new immigrants, and Irish women came to dominate the city's produce business. Hughes's sister Angela, a nun with the Sisters of Charity, became a role model for Irish women as founder of Saint Vincent's hospital.

Hughes dismissed what New York City officials called "charity" – warehousing the poor in the subsistence almshouses until they died, usually of typhus, typhoid fever, consumption or cholera – as "Soupery." Instead, Hughes imported church groups like the St. Vincent de Paul Society, a group of laymen who visited prisons, organized youth groups and taught reading and writing. Whenever they provided food, clothing or shelter, they required recipients to work in return. The Sisters of Mercy worked closely with the St. Vincent de Paul Society, visiting the city's almshouses and prisons and urging the women there to find work and follow church teachings.

Two generations following the influx of Irish immigrants, the Irish proportion of arrests for violent crime had dropped to less than 10% from 60%, Irish children were entering the priesthood and the convent, the professions, politics, show business and commerce. In 1890, some 30% of the city's teachers were Irish women, and the Irish literacy rate exceeded 90%. With the 1880 election of shipping magnate William Grace as mayor, the Irish assumed control of city politics.

Today many people sneer at the kind of faith, discipline and work that Archbishop Hughes preached and practiced among New York's underclass. Those who would preach about today's underclass, however, could learn a great deal from the successes his efforts produced."

As you can see, "Dagger John" was quite a man. I wish I possessed just a segment of his courage. People like him make us realize we are truly standing on the shoulders of giants.

With every good wish,

Fr. Dan Madigan

Modesto Bee photograph

Abandoned baby mourned

Stanislaus County Deputy Coroner Judy Barter carries a coffin bearing the body of "David Joseph Doe" on Wednesday. Thirty mourners gathered for a service at Lakewood Memorial Park in Hughson. The body was found in December at Co-Compost Facility west of Modesto; the mother is unknown.

Dear Friends:

I love animals. I keep a number of dogs and an adorable donkey. Money can purchase creatures like these, but it's only kindness that will make the dogs wag their tails and the donkey talk in her own peculiar way.

Jesus Christ was a soft-hearted man. He openly sobbed when Lazarus died. He cried over the condition of Jerusalem. He had tremendous compassion for everyday folks, and His empathy for the poor was nothing short of enormous.

All of us know that when our heart stops, our body dies. What we don't seem to recognize is that when compassion disappears from a community, its soul goes right along with it.

In the last number of years I feel much sensitivity and compassion has dissipated from the U.S. scene. I base my judgment on articles I read in national, secular, and religious newsprint. The void created is quickly filled with severity and harshness of thinking.

Those of us who have had a deep fear experience in our life can testify to its paralyzing effect. Some animals freeze at the sight of their predators. While awaiting His persecutors, Jesus sweated blood through the pores of His flesh. Deep fear can cripple the bravest of souls.

Many months ago I watched a TV program which has stayed with me ever since. It was about young teenage girls abandoning their babies. **Abandonment usually brought death to the baby.** A gruesome story for TV. Contemptuous outrage by the community. And twenty-five-to-life for the frightened child-like mom.

We here at SFBS deal with over 15,000 infants and their moms each year. I believe that we should have some program readily available for those who wish to have a baby but still stay anonymous. To meet this end please pray that our State will put something very practical together.

Have a very blessed Easter Season. And please remember us by way of a donation. After all, we only operate because of your generosity.

With every good wish,

Fr. Dan Madigan

Dear Friends:

Many times we have a tendency to believe that we are self-made people. But in moments of total honesty we know that our lives and our characters have been shaped by many great folks such as parents, siblings, extended family, teachers and religious personnel.

When I think of my mom, the words of Mother Machree come to mind.

> *I kiss the dear fingers so toil worn for me,*
> *Oh, God bless you and keep you, Mother Machree!*

When I think of my dad, the words of Edgar Guest flash across my mind:

> *Only a dad but he gives his all.*
> *To smooth the way for his children small,*
> *Doing with courage stern and grim,*
> *The deeds that his father did for him.*

When I think of my brothers and sister who remained on the farms, I am very much reminded of the story of Albrecht Durer:

> *Back in the fifteenth century, in a tiny village near Nuremberg, lived a family with eighteen children. Eighteen! In order merely to keep food on the table for this mob, the father and head of the household, a goldsmith by profession, worked almost eighteen hours a day at his trade and any other paying chore he could find in the neighborhood.*
>
> *Despite their seemingly hopeless condition, two of the Durer's children had a dream. They both wanted to pursue their talent for art, but they knew full well that their father would never be financially able to send either of them to Nuremberg to study at the Academy.*
>
> *After many long discussions at night in their crowded bed, the two boys finally worked out a pact. They would toss a coin. The loser would go down into the nearby mines and, with his earnings, support his brother while he attended the academy. Then, when that brother who won the toss completed his studies, in four years, he would support the other brother at the academy, either with sales of his artwork or, if necessary, also by laboring in the mines.*
>
> *They tossed a coin on a Sunday morning after church. Albrecht Durer won the toss and went off to Nuremberg.*
>
> *Albert went down into the dangerous mines and, for the next four years, financed his brother, whose work at the academy was almost an immediate sensation. Albrecht's etchings, his woodcuts, and his oils were far better than those of most of his professors, and by the time he graduated, he was beginning to earn considerable fees for his commissioned works.*
>
> *When the young artist returned to his village, the Durer family held a festive dinner on their lawn to celebrate Albrecht's triumphant homecoming. After a long and memorable meal, punctuated with music and laughter, Albrecht rose from his honored position at the head of the table to drink a toast to his beloved brother for the years of sacrifice that had enabled Albrecht to fulfill his ambition. His*

closing words were, 'And now, Albert, blessed brother of mine, now it is your turn. Now you can go to Nuremberg to pursue your dream, and I will take care of you.'

All heads turned in eager expectation to the far end of the table where Albert sat, tears streaming down his pale face, shaking his lowered head from side to side while he sobbed and repeated, over and over, 'No...no...no...no.'

Finally, Albert rose and wiped the tears from his cheeks. He glanced down the long table at the faces he loved, and then, holding his hands close to his right cheek, he said softly, 'No, brother, I cannot go to Nuremberg. It is too late for me. Look..look what four years in the mines have done to my hands! The bones in every finger have been smashed at least once, and lately I have been suffering from arthritis so badly in my right hand that I cannot even hold a glass to return your toast, much less make delicate lines on parchment or canvas with a pen or a brush. No, brother..for me it is too late.'

More than 450 years have passed. By now, Albrecht Durer's hundreds of masterful portraits, pen and silverpoint sketches, watercolors, charcoals, woodcuts, and copper engravings hang in every great museum in the world, but the odds are great that you, like most people, are familiar with only one of Albrecht Durer's works. More than merely being familiar with it, you very well may have a reproduction hanging in your home or office.

*One day, to pay homage to Albert for all that he had sacrificed, Albrecht Durer painstakingly drew his brother's abused hands with palms together and thin fingers stretched skyward. He called his powerful drawing simply 'Hands,' but the entire world almost immediately opened their hearts to his great masterpiece and renamed his tribute of love **"The Praying Hands."***

Friends, let us always remember. No person is an island. No person makes it on his own. We all need help. We all need friends. We all need a hand-up. We need mentors. We need to mentor.

So, be kind, charitable and non-judgmental people and always build as many bridges as you can for others to cross.

If you can send a donation this time of year please do so. The summer months are our leanest from a financial point of view.

With every good wish,

Fr. Dan Madigan

Dear Friends:

On May 2ⁿᵈ seventy-six people traveled with me to Ireland. Practically all were disciples of SFBS.

The Emerald Isle looks great. Its economy is booming. New homes spring up all over the countryside. Construction cranes loom over many of the towns.

Euphoria is in the air. Newfound prosperity is everywhere. The Celtic tiger is out of his cage and roams the island. He is also recruiting in New York, Boston, Chicago and San Francisco and inviting his professional and skillful cubs to come back home.

Experience has shown me that poverty is like the shy member of a family who has not measured up to the standards of his siblings. Poverty lurks in the shadows. Poverty keeps to itself and is very much allowed to do so by its prosperous sisters and brothers.

This is true in the USA. This is true in Ireland. Prosperity always shies away from poverty. Prosperity is very much ashamed of poverty.

In the U.S. who visits our cities' pocket of poverty? Who takes vacations in dirt-poor Appalachia? Who drops in on our rural poor?

After I said goodbye to my traveling friends at Shannon Airport I returned to my family home and spoke to boyhood friends who pointed out to me the gaping holes in Ireland's booming economy. I talked to farmers who filled me in on last year's severe winter. They told me about the starving cattle and the rock bottom beef and milk prices. They told me of the necessary emigration from the farms and the so-called govern- ment assistance programs that had run amok.

So, as I have often mentioned in my newsletters, our view of life depends on the hill on which we stand or the tunnel in which we live.

To be a truly just person we need to know what exactly is going on in life. To be a kind and charitable human being, we have to own an open empathetic heart.

With every good wish,

Fr. Dan Madigan

Dear Friends:

I never considered myself much of a philosopher, theologian or liturgist, but I always felt I knew how to **teach and preach.** Teaching is educating the mind. Preaching is educating the heart. At SFBS we do both.

An old Turkish proverb says, "if you don't know where you are going, any road will get you there." SFBS was fortunate from its inception as it possessed crystal clear vision of its mission and the ability of communicating it to the Sacramento community.

SFBS also refused to belly up to the government trough for its existence and avoided heavy dependency on the ecclesiastical structure.

SFBS never compromised principles for results. It knew that success meant hard work, long hours and uncompromising endurance. It paid that price. It demanded excellence of itself, and it quickly gained the confidence of the Sacramento community.

Because of this, volunteers came in droves. Money flowed in with consistency and word got out among the poor that SFBS was a haven of compassion and permanence at its two outlets, Oak Park and Del Paso Heights.

Now as we stand on the doorstep of our silver jubilee, SFBS is proud of its ability to interact daily with its thousand or so clients who show up for help. SFBS accomplishes all this through the assets it has accumulated over the years.

Our assets:

- A 30,000 square food headquarters (formerly Arata Bros.) located in Oak Park.
- A fifteen-year-old triple wide trailer, "Madigan Ranchero," at Norwood and Hayes in Del Paso Heights.
- Ongoing regional support.
- A dedicated board of directors, most of whom have been with SFBS since its inception.
- A staff of twenty five people who possess a high level of leadership skills.
- Twelve dwellings in Oak Park for housing the homeless.
- A fleet of trucks for transportation purposes.
- Room size refrigerators and freezers for food storage.
- A 3,000 square foot Community Learning Center located adjacent to SFBS campus.
- An annual income of one and one half million dollars which flows in from individuals (54%), local business (26%), fundraising events (14%) and government (6%.)
- An organization that has learned to daily walk the razor's edge of being close to broke, while at the same time being able to cope with the stress that this type of operation brings with it.
- Presently SFBS owns all of its properties and equipment and is totally debt free.

With every good wish,

Fr. Dan Madigan

Dear Friends:

I guess the older we get the more we reminisce. At least, that's what's happening to me.

In the 1960s **Mrs. Schilling lived with her mom, Mrs. Carroll,** in a dilapidated little home in Del Paso Heights. To me both ladies seemed the same age. Of course, this was not at all the case. Mrs. Carroll was in her 90's, her daughter in her 60's.

On a hundred-plus degree afternoon Mrs. Schilling called me and said she felt her mother was dead. I rushed to their little home and found Mrs. Carroll sitting lifeless in a rocking chair.

Those were not the days of 911 and I knew little about calling ambulances. So I anointed the dear woman and asked her daughter if they owned a fan. She showed me a heavy duty commercial piece of machinery with a broken plug. I sat at the kitchen table and succeeded in fixing it with a knife. Once I got this blower aimed at Mrs. Carroll, she woke up and said, "Hi, Fr. Madigan, isn't it a hot day you are out in."

I specifically remember one evening dropping in on these ladies as they were having their evening dinner. The sparseness of their meal haunted me as I journeyed back to the rectory to join my pastor, Fr. John Terwilliger, for our well prepared dinner.

After some years Mrs. Carroll died. Mrs. Schilling was totally lost. She used to come by the rectory often to tell me she was lonely and to ask for some cigarettes. As I was a smoker then I always had some to share with her. Suddenly she stopped coming. I tried to track her down but to no avail. The years went by and I was transferred from Del Paso Heights to Sacred Heart Church at 39th and J Streets.

While at Sacred Heart I got a call from a local funeral home asking if I would officiate at a county burial at Mount Calvary Cemetery in the north area.

The morning of the burial was beautiful. The sun was shining bright and the air was crisp and cold. The snow on the Sierra Nevada seemed ever so near. The mortician together with two gentlemen from the cemetery and myself carried the casket from the hearse to the grave. The gentlemen from the cemetery left and the mortician and I waited for a County social worker who, by the way, never showed up.

The mortician and I talked about how terrible it was for a human being to have no one present at her burial except for two strangers. But strangers we were not as I was about to find out.

As I began the burial prayers I asked the mortician for the name of the deceased. He pulled out the clergyman's card and handed it to me. It was Eileen Schilling. I had to excuse myself and walk away for a while. It took me some time to gather myself together. This sacred occurrence really got to me.

So, Eileen Schilling and May Carroll, I am sure you are with God. I ask you both to please intercede to Our Heavenly Father for us, the volunteers, donors and staff of SFBS.

With every good wish,

Fr. Dan Madigan

253

Dear Friends:

Recently a friend of mine came by our church at Clarksburg. He had his six-year-old daughter with him. He removed her bicycle from their automobile and put on her helmet. Then looking her straight in the eye said, *"Katie, you have lots of room in this parking lot **so now enjoy riding your bicycle.**"*

Katie indeed did well with her little mode of transportation. As her dad and I stood talking, I noticed his eyes were glued to every move his daughter made. Indeed he was like a greyhound ready to spring from its racing kennel if anything happened to his beloved Katie.

The scene reminded me of a scripture quotation from the Deuteronomy, 32.11:

> *"As an eagle incites its nestlings forth*
> *by hovering over its brood,*
> *So he spread his wings to receive them*
> *and bore them up on his pinions."*

Every bird has to entice and persuade its young to leave the security of the nest. Venturing forth into the unknown is a very scary moment for baby and parents.

Eagles build their nests (aeries) in very high places. When a young eaglet gets the courage to attempt its maiden voyage, its parents fly underneath it to prevent it from falling to the ground. That is why the above Scripture passage says that the parents collect their chicks on their pinions (extended wings.)

At SFBS we teach somewhat in the same manner as the eagle does. We do not spend as much time in teaching cold, hard facts for the mind to dwell on, as we do with the gentle mentoring of the person.

Our mentors are extremely kind and patient. They walk hand-in-hand with their nestlings. They build whatever bridges need to be erected. They go to great extremes not to "extinguish the smoldering wick" or "crush the broken reed."

Our country is full of prisons. Our society is convinced that punishment deters crime, but Christ thinks differently. According to Him, compassion is the tool to use. So, SFBS hangs in with the good Lord's gentle approach. Surprise! Surprise! It works.

With every good wish,

Fr. Dan Madigan

Dear Friends:

I have two donkeys, **Jessie the female is ten years old** and Joshua the male is two.

They are highly intelligent animals. They refuse to be commanded blindly but are most cooperative with any common sense request.

The reputation that donkeys are stubborn and stupid is ill-founded. Just as bad craftsmen blame their tools, so do poor handlers blame their donkeys.

The word "ass" is the proper name for a donkey. It is used exclusively in the Bible. However, nowadays translations are using the word donkey because of the slang meaning the word ass carries with it.

Donkeys love their dust baths. They take them several times a day. They live between 40 and 50 years. They like treats such as candy, fruits, bread and vegetables. They love their owners and will salute them from a long distance with a loud bray.

Now for some family terminology. Ass, donkey and burro are synonymous. A jennet is a female donkey. A jack is a male donkey. A mule's mom is a horse and its dad is a donkey. A hinny's mom is a donkey and its dad is a horse. By the way, mules and hinnys are sterile.

I recently heard a story of a donkey that fell in a deep well. As the donkey was old and the well was dry and non-productive, the farmer decided to fill it in with dirt and thus bury his poor old donkey.

However, the donkey had a different agenda. Every time the farmer threw in a wheelbarrow of dirt the donkey shook it off himself and stepped up on it. By continuing to shake off the dirt and step on it the donkey eventually walked out of the well.

Friends, let's take a lesson from this wise old donkey. When we find people firing negative stuff at us, let's just keep stepping on it, while at the same time hanging on to our own integrity and decency. In that way we too will eventually step up out of our well of misfortune.

Thanksgiving is almost upon us. Mid-November to mid-January is my favorite time of year. The weather is usually cold, but fires are lighting and hearts are warm. It's that time of year when people think more about their families, think more about the poor, think more about God, and thus become more compassionate, tolerant and lovable.

Please help SFBS to the best of your ability.

With every good wish,

Fr. Dan Madigan

258

Dear Friends:

I have always been a night owl. I love to stroll the church grounds when darkness has descended and when the air is crisp and the vineyards are asleep.

When I step out my back door the silence is broken by my donkeys, mules and dogs. They await their nightly visit. They expect their bedtime treats.

Sometimes the solitude is again broken by the serenading of coyotes. They howl and yip and with their changing notes successfully give the impression that they are many.

However, this may not be the case. It's early February and it's mating season for the alpha pair of the pack. Their howling is rejoicing. The other four to six pack members are hunting. For them it's the celibate life. That's the way it is.

Pups will be born in late April or early May. The pack will rear them. Howling will again occur in September when the entire family is training the pups to hunt.

Mark Twain said, *"The coyote is a living, breathing allegory of Want. He is always hungry. He is always poor, out of luck and friendless."*

I once watched a coyote at Yosemite. It was daytime and he should have been asleep. Instead he was sneaking around on the outskirts of the crowd awaiting an opportunity to snatch some food. This sorrow-looking creature had sold out to dependency.

When one is at the bottom of the barrel, it's easy to sell out to dependency. Bureaucracy loves dependent obedient people   They are so easy to handle.

SFBS is different. It promotes independence. Having given people sufficient fish to strengthen them, SFBS then hands them a fishing pole and says, "Let's go use this instrument".

Bellying up to the bureaucratic trough is something SFBS has never done. Remaining free and independent of this entanglement, SFBS is in a position to free others.

You Sacramentans like our style. You have stood behind us these past 25 years. Stood behind us financially. Stood behind us with your volunteer hours. Best of all, stood behind us with your total belief, prayers and good wishes.

With every good wish,

Fr. Dan Madigan

Dear Friends:

My Dad was a farmer. A gentle, soft spoken, grade-school educated person, he possessed the essence of integrity and a truckload of common sense.

We siblings loved him dearly. He constantly shared with us stories and his home spun sayings.

"Never throw water on a drowning rat" he would tell us. From this saying we quickly learned that we must at all times help our fellow man and indeed any and all of God's creatures.

"Always feed the rooster" he used to say. Apparently as a youngster he watched a neighbor lady feed her hens. While doing so, she held her rooster under her arm. The hens she felt deserved food as they gave her eggs but the rooster deserved nothing as his services were not needed. Dad thought this was cruel. Using this incident he instilled in us youngsters compassion and acceptance for all of God's creatures irrespective of their ability at productivity.

Dad always spoke with the utmost respect about his parents and grandparents. His grandfather, Michael, and Michael's brother, Fr. Denis, lived through the famine. At that time, if you turned your back on your religion, the English fed you soup. If you expressed interest in joining the British army, you were handed a bright new shilling and embraced like a brother. If you wanted to show respect for your landlord, you wore a white feather in your cap. Dad always assured us that our ancestors had never succumbed to the unjust and alien authority they lived under. They held their heads high and never sold out to the establishment of that day.

Dad, thank you for the wisdom you shared with me. I promise *I will never throw water on a drowning rat. I will always feed the rooster. I will never drink the soup. I will never take the shilling.* Also, be assured *I will never wear the white feather.*

Friends – you are wonderful and generous folks and I thank you from the bottom of my heart for all your kindness to the poor through SFBS. Also, I want to thank you for all the friendship and love you extend to me personally.

With every good wish,

Fr. Dan Madigan

Dear Friends:

John Newton was born in London on July 24, 1725. **His mother was a very religious lady and taught her young son all about God and the Christian way of life.**

John's mom died when he was only seven. John soon forgot all about his mother's teaching. He went off to sea and became the captain of a slave trading ship.

The story goes that his crew became so disgusted with the depravity of his behavior that once when he fell overboard, while in a drunken stupor, they rescued him by throwing a harpoon into him and pulling him back into the ship. From that day on John Newton walked with a limp.

It was during a violent storm at sea that John reverted to his mom's teaching and became very close to God. "Amazing Grace" is probably his best known hymn.

> *"Amazing grace! How sweet the sound,*
> *That saved a wretch like me!*
> *I once was lost, but now am found,*
> *Was blind, but now I see.*
>
> *'Twas grace that taught my heart to fear,*
> *And grace my fears relieved;*
> *How precious did that grace appear*
> *The hour I first believed!*
>
> *The Lord has promised good to me,*
> *God's word my hope secures;*
> *God will my shield and portion be*
> *As long as life endures.*
>
> *Through many dangers, toils and snares,*
> *I have already come;*
> *'Tis grace has brought me safe thus far,*
> *And grace will lead me home."*

Happy Easter to you. Please remember that the Good Lord is always willing to do for us what he did for John Newton. All we have to do is ask.

With every good wish,

Fr. Dan Madigan

Dear Friends:

What causes cruelty? Rape? Violence? Dysfunctional living?

Most people believe it's the apple itself that decides to go bad.

The prison system is set up to warehouse these rotten apples. The mind of many people is to eliminate these hard-core criminals completely.

The government and most churches play a low profile in regard to these issues and generally cater to the general consensus.

Christ seems to stand alone on the issue. Compassion will work He tells us. It will. It will. It will. Capital punishment, He says, is wrong.

SFBS says, *"A stitch in time saves nine"*. In other words, let's get to folks when they are young. After all, seventy percent of adult prisoners are graduates of the juvenile system.

It takes one million to house a lifer, and one hundred thousand dollars to build one cell. Despite this knowledge, California has built twenty prisons and two universities in the last ten years.

Violence begets violence. Everyone knows that. Fires are not quenched with gasoline. Everyone knows that. Yet our widespread irrational yearning to inflict punishment is gaining ground every day.

Why not try Christ's way? Why not stop piling humiliation, shame and inferiority on the dysfunctional? Why not try **promoting education, skill, self respect and esteem for everyone?**

I appeal to all SFBS supporters to strive at becoming more gentle, kind and less judgmental. Please join me and together we will promote kindness and downplay the toughness I feel is presently sweeping over our land.

Friends, hold on to the real Christ, the totally compassionate One. He will work wonders in your life.

With every good wish,

Fr. Dan Madigan

Dear Friends:

Working with the poor does not give one a complete picture of their plight. Living with them does.

For fourteen years I resided in Oak Park. My bedroom window overlooked Broadway's busy thoroughfare. An all-night bar with open double doors sat directly across the street from my little nest. **Bikers arrived almost every night** and usually stayed until dawn.

I have vivid memories of trying to sleep in a non-air conditioned room while listening to the shouts of revelry intertwined with profanity that spewed through those open doors.

A veteran policeman told me there was little they could do to stop this behavior. However, he assured me that situations like this always take care of themselves. How right he was. After lots of fights, some stabbings and a murder, the place closed down.

At the same time, our church operated Oak Park's only grade school. During my stint there, a new principal was having difficulty with two little siblings. He decided to walk them to their nearby home and talk to their mom.

Later a devastated principal returned to my office. The obscene graffiti, the padlocked gates and windows, the dingy dimly lit apartment and the devastated mom he encountered were more than he could handle. He slouched in the armchair and asked me, "Do you fully realize what we are up against? And, if so, how do you think we are going to cope with this environment?"

Well, with God's wonderful help we did cope with it. In a little over six months (January 17) SFBS will be celebrating its 25th anniversary.

I am extremely proud of our agency. Our home, the former Arata grocery store, now sees almost as many people as it did in its heyday as a grocery store.

Thank you all for your kindness and goodness to the work we do. It's great to live each day knowing we are making a difference to many, many people.

With every good wish,

Fr. Dan Madigan

Dear Friends:

As the starving French people huddled outside the gates of the Bastille, Marie Antoinette said, *"Let them eat cake"*.

Historians disagree as to whether she was blatantly naïve or extremely cruel.

Last year as a SFBS volunteer picked up **a barrel of used tennis shoes** from a local sporting store, he overheard a customer say, *"What do the poor need tennis shoes for?"*

SFBS staff still disagrees as to whether this person was extremely naïve, totally uncaring or just visiting us from another planet.

Yes, the poor, just like the rest of us, do need shoes. They also need food, clothing, housing and interaction with friendly faces and helping hands. Thank God, because of your involvement with us, SFBS is able to provide much to the poor.

There is an old Irish saying which goes something like this, *"Those bringing sunshine to the lives of others surely can't be keeping it from themselves"*. How true that is. Our Lord says the same thing in many different ways. *"We reap what we sow"*. *"We will be measured by the measure we use on others"*. *"The cup of cold water we give to others will not go unnoticed"*.

Please pray for our organization. You are a part of it. Some of you have joined us recently, others over the years and a sizeable cadre of you have been with us since our inception almost twenty-five years ago.

Pray to God that our level of honesty and dedication and delivery will continue to grow in a manner in keeping with the thinking of Our Blessed Lord.

With every good wish,

Fr. Dan Madigan

Dear Friends:

Pat and I are life long buddies. Under the auspices of Catholic Charities, Pat ran an outstanding social service agency for fifteen years in another state.

Recently he wrote to me saying he was moving on to other work. His reason, *"We have lost the soul of our mission in favor of a growing emphasis on non-essential activities. This is my assessment and I do not foresee us 'putting the genie' back in the bottle"*.

Yes, indeed, it's easy to lose the God-given integrity that holds the fabric of any group together. Families can lose it. Schools can lose it. Churches can lose it. And, yes, social service agencies can lose it.

As my friend Pat says, once the genie is out of the bottle, it's well-nigh impossible for the same team to put a decent workable spirit back together again.

At SFBS we instill into our staff that they are not working at a job but doing missionary work. We let them know that we are responding to a higher calling. Integrity is not negotiable. They must always know what they are doing. Love what they are doing, and believe in what they are doing.

To keep us all true to our mission, I often ask for prayers for SFBS. So far, we are doing well, our genie is still in our bottle.

At the moment Peter Berghuis is the driving force and dynamo behind our organization. I am Peter's advisor, The Board of Directors' visionary and the donors' emissary. While many see my role as fundraiser, I don't view it that way. **My job is making friends for SFBS.** Having done this, I believe friends donate and when possible they volunteer.

With every good wish,

Fr. Dan Madigan

Dear Friends:

As a youngster I watched the owner of **a very hungry dog** tether it to a tree and then place a portion of bread beyond its reach. The hungry dog struggled and struggled to get that food. It extended its paw as far as possible but the bread was carefully placed inches beyond its toenails. I did nothing to stop the persecution. I guess I did not have the guts.

Nor do I exempt myself from critter cruelty. Once when given the job of feeding a neighbors ducks, I found the creatures ravenous. I mixed their feed of bran and hot water and laid it out for them on the ground. It was way too hot. When the poor creatures grabbed a bite they had to run to a nearby puddle of water for relief. I remember watching those ducks bang into each other and knock each other over as they rushed to the water and rushed back for food. It seemed funny to me at the time but my feelings changed as this incident has haunted me for the past fifty years.

The feast of St. Francis is almost upon us. On that day I will bless all of God's creatures. The place and time of the blessings are attached.

Mahatma Gandhi said, *"The greatness of a nation can be judged by the way its animals are treated"*. At our last blessing I was pleasantly surprised by the outgoing, lovable personalities of all the animals. As I blessed them individually, they were very affectionate toward their owners and equally accepting of me. I can assure you that during that ceremony I got more than one big wet kiss from those lovely creatures.

One day in the not too distant future I would like to start a non-profit sanctuary for donkeys and mules. I pray often that God will send along a generous donor who will come up with about twenty acres of agricultural land so we can put together an oasis of happiness for these lovable animals. By the way, I have a huge barn that will house these critters.

With every good wish,

Fr. Dan Madigan

Dear Friends:

I watch very little TV. The news, 48 hours, Nightline, 20/20, Sixty Minutes. That's about it.

From one of the above programs, I learned that the top criteria used in the choosing of our country's vice president is their lack of potential liability.

On the back burner sits the wonderful qualities like character, integrity, spirituality, leadership, skill at communicating, and talent at motivating. Instead, the absence of potential liability rules the roost.

In the late sixties and right through the seventies, college students flocked to the helping professions. The schools of social work, nursing, psychology and sociology were full.

Medicine, dentistry and the law were also viewed favorably because of their pro bono work. Legal clinics and storefront medical outlets were opened in many cities.

Then came the eighties. Commerce gained a new luster. Fame and wealth got back in the saddle. MBAs and entrepreneurs suddenly became idols. So it is today for a very large segment of people. For them the lure of material wealth and its commitment status is irresistible.

Our society is paying a big price for where we are now. Employer/employee loyalty is gone. Managed care took out the benevolent doctor. Government cuts destroyed many social agencies. A huge segment of the legal profession has lost its soul. Potential liability has frightened the church into silence. Yes, indeed, common sense, down-to-earth problem-solving professionals are getting very scarce.

Are today's family physicians urging their sons and daughters to go to medical school? Studies say no. Is the social work field attracting the top of the graduating high school class? Schools say no. Are priests and nuns stepping forward as they used to? I don't think so.

All this is happening because we threw common sense, down-to-earth compassion and backbone right out the window. Until they are brought back, greed and liability, with their **frozen fields of harshness,** will continue to rule the roost.

Take care. God bless. And do hold on to your compassionate heart.

With every good wish,

Fr. Dan Madigan

Dear Friends:

I am now 62 pushing 63. Old enough to reminisce of bygone days. Fuzzy about yesterday but crystal clear of my youthful escapades.

I was a boarder all through high school and seminary. Escaping for Christmas from those cold militaristic institutions into the warmth of a loving family was wonderful.

Like all our rural neighbors the Madigans were simple folks. Long winter evenings were spent around the fire. Conversation dominated the evenings that ran from about 5:00 p.m. to midnight. Visiting neighbors, ghost stories, card games, scalding hot tea and brandy soaked plum pudding also played a big part in the camaraderie.

Prior to Christmas all households purchased a number of large candles. Carved turnips served as candle-sticks and candles were lit for the entire Christmas Season (Dec. 25 to Jan. 6.)

Last week a friend of mine gave me a book titled "More Irish Stories for Christmas." Little did the giver realize that I know John B. Keane, the book's author.

John writes, *"The spirit of Christmas has survived the Stalins, the Hitlers and the Mussolinis and all those too who have perpetrated injustices since the birth of Christ. It has survived human greed and human jealousy and every human failing one cares to mention".*

He adds, *"Don't ever be ashamed to be weepy or sentimental about Christmas because you might not get the chance during the year ahead to show your humanity to the world and what the hell good is humanity if it's suffocated by caution!"*

Like John B. Keane, **Christmas** to me has always been the essence of compassion, gentleness, kindness and forgiveness.

Please hold on to these great qualities and don't let the harshness, severity and legalistic caution and fears of other people's minds influence your life.

My prayer for you during this wonderful season is that the Child Jesus will strengthen your own inner goodness.

With every good wish,

Fr. Dan Madigan

WELCOME

St. Joseph's
Catholic
Church

Fr. Dan Madigan
Pastor

CONCLUSION

Oftentimes I worry about the things I forgot to do in life. Things I promised people I would take care of but didn't. Appointments I may have missed, or phone messages that somehow got lost and not returned. If you are one of my victims I sincerely apologize and I will do this through the following beautiful poem that was written by William Butler Yeats about an old priest during the famine time in Ireland.

The old priest Peter Gilligan
Was weary night and day;
For half his flock were in their beds,
Or under green sods lay.

Once while he nodded on a chair
At the moth-hour of eve,
Another poor man sent for him,
And he began to grieve.

"I have no rest, nor joy, nor peace,
For people die and die."
And after cried he, "God forgive!
My body spake, not I!"

And then, half-lying on the chair,
He knelt, prayed, fell asleep;
And the moth-hour went from the fields,
And stars began to peep.

They slowly into millions grew,
And leaves shook in the wind;
And God covered the world with shade,
And whispered to mankind.

Upon the time of sparrow chirp
When the moths came once more,
The old priest Peter Gilligan
Stood upright on the floor.

"Mavrone, mavrone! The man has died.
While I slept on the chair."
He roused his horse out of its sleep,
And rode with little care.

He rode now as he never rode,
By rocky lane and fen;
The sick man's wife opened the door;
"Father, you come again!"

"And is the poor man dead?" he cried.
"He died an hour ago."
The old priest Peter Gilligan
In grief swayed to and fro.

"When you were gone, he turned and died
As merry as a bird."
The old priest Peter Gilligan
He knelt him at that word.

"He who hath made the night of stars
For souls, who tire and bleed,
Sent one of His great angels down
To help me in my need.

He who is wrapped in purple robes,
With planets in His care,
Had pity on the least of things
Asleep upon a chair."

287